Empowering School Leaders

Personal Political Power for School Board Members and Administrators

Joel Blackwell

The Grassroots Guy

Rowman & Littlefield Education
Lanham, Maryland • Toronto • Oxford
2006

Published in the United States of America
by Rowman & Littlefield Education
A Division of Rowman & Littlefield Publishers, Inc.
A wholly owned subsidary of The Rowman & Littlefield Publishing Group, Inc.
4501 Forbes Boulevard, Suite 200, Lanham, Maryland 20706
www.rowmaneducation.com

PO Box 317
Oxford
OX2 9RU, UK

British Library Cataloguing in Publication Information Available

Library of Congress Cataloging-in-Publication Data

Blackwell, Joel, 1944–
  Empowering school leaders : personal political power for school
board members and administrators / Joel Blackwell.
    p. cm.
  ISBN 13: 978-1-57886-423-2 (hardcover : alk. paper)
  ISBN 13: 978-1-57886-349-5 (pbk. : alk. paper)
  ISBN 10: 1-57886-423-2 (hardcover : alk. paper)
  ISBN 10: 1-57886-349-X (pbk. : alk. paper)
  1. School management and organization—Political aspects.
2. Education—Political aspects. I. Title.

LB2805.B5633   2006
379.1′531—dc22

                              2005033021

∞ ™ The paper used in this publication meets the minimum requirements of
American National Standard for Information Sciences—Permanence of
Paper for Printed Library Materials, ANSI/NISO Z39.48-1992.
Manufactured in the United States of America.

Contents

Introduction

Empowering School Leaders: Personal Political Power for School Board Members and Administrators is divided into two parts. Part I contains interviews with ordinary people, paid professional lobbyists, and politicians. Part II details how you can become an effective part of the political process working in tandem with people like those you meet in part I. Finally, four appendixes contain miscellaneous examples and advice.

Empowering School Leaders is about getting results on political issues in education. It is not for "casework." If you have a personal problem that affects only you, the staff of your elected officials will help eagerly. That's their job. So if you aren't getting results, you probably want something you don't deserve. Get therapy.

Issues, on the other hand, are things that might be decided by a vote in your city council, county commission, legislature, or Congress. One important operating principle: Don't expect politicians to pay attention to you if you represent just one person with a need or good idea that only affects you. They don't have time to devote to such matters because there are too many good ideas that have widespread support from broad-based organizations called special interest groups.

You will often hear politicians, even experienced ones, deriding the power of "special interest groups." The newspapers and television routinely portray them as a human version of the AIDS virus, a plague upon the republic that needs to be eradicated. I hope when you've finished this book you have a different view. I hope you will see how the Constitution supports and enables "special interest groups," and what an important and positive contribution they make to our democracy. In fact, our democracy is designed and intended to foster the formation of special interest groups.

The next time you hear a politician railing against "special interest groups," ask him or her this: "Which special interest groups have too much power and what would you do to curtail it? AARP? NRA? Teachers? School boards? Realtors? Boy Scouts? Catholic Church? Insurance agents?

Fact is, any honest politician will tell you the government, and certainly the politicians, couldn't function without special interest lobbying groups with their volunteer and professional staff.

In education, lobbying groups represent teachers, school board members, principals and other administrators, and parent–teacher groups, for example. Then you have related organizations of bus drivers and food preparers. If you aren't part of a special interest group, join one or form one. It takes an organization to demonstrate widespread support, build consensus, and create enough political weight to make something happen.

An element that potentially has the power to radically improve the education system is missing in action. Parents. They are difficult to mobilize about education policy. A typical PTA will raise thousands of dollars for playground equipment but never approach a politician to get more money for books. Parents, like many other Americans, are politically AWOL.

A national PTA lobbyist estimated perhaps 10% of member parents engage in any kind of advocacy. My hunch is that's wishful thinking. PTA, like other parent organizations, has not earned the right to be taken seriously in the political arena.

If you would like to change that, keep reading. The following pages explain how things work in real life. If you don't like the system, change it. On some structural issues, such as money, many politicians and lobbyists will agree with you. I probably agree with you. But for today, I'm trying to help you get what you want from the system as it exists, using tried and proven techniques.

Part I tells you what you need to know through interviews with people who have deep experience in legislative lobbying and politics: elected officeholders, lobbyists, and volunteer advocates.

Part II collects this wisdom and outlines, step by step, what you need to do to get what you want from government. The goal is to help you see that you can have significant influence on public policy and then tell you what you must do to exert that influence.

BASIC CONCEPTS

- Our political system is not designed to decide who is right and who is wrong. It is designed to decide who has a majority.
- If you can't prove that lots of people are with you, you will fail.
- There are no right or wrong positions in politics, just decisions made by human beings for good reasons or bad reasons, or out of indifference.
- If you have the votes in the legislature or Congress, you're right. If you don't, you're wrong.
- No political decision is permanent; the fat lady never sings.

I came to understand (and people like elected superintendents and school board members also understand) an important dynamic of politics. When you run for office, you learn there is a special relationship between politicians and the people who put them in office—the voters in their district. Elected officials lust for their approval. They are the most important people in the world, and you must pay attention to them. They are your customers, and if they don't buy what you are selling, you will go out of business.

People who have been elected always listen to the people who can vote for them. Those potential voters have enormous power if they express themselves. Most never do.

When I ran for the state legislature in North Carolina, I identified the important issues, illuminated them in new ways, and proposed sensible solutions. In so doing, I held my opponent to 76% of the vote. I learned a lot about how politicians feel about the people who can vote for them and I hope to pass it on to you.

My goal is to get every concerned American to speak, as a representative or member of an organized group, to the people they vote for, just as the writers of the Constitution intended. If we do that, we can solve every problem the nation faces.

I fear that Americans will sink into cynicism and doubt about our political system. Our system is in danger because too many people are political dropouts. The presentation of politics in newspapers and television feeds negativity and gives people an easy excuse to shun political activity. To an outsider, it all seems about money, power, and often sex. Our system is not perfect by any stretch, but it works for those who work it. People aren't left out; they drop out.

In the 2004 presidential election, more than half of registered voters turned out in many places. But in most elections, only 20% to 40% of Americans vote; an even smaller number makes meaningful contact with an elected officeholder about an issue. My grassroots poll in 2000 found that about 13% of Americans have contributed money or time to a politician. That so few people vote, that far fewer write letters or make phone calls to politicians, and almost none give money or time means that those who do wield disproportionate power. People who write letters, make contributions and phone calls, or give time to politicians form a political elite that drives public policy.

My experience and that of many other political professionals tells me that less than 1% of Americans communicate often enough and effectively enough to influence policy. You can be in that political elite.

It amazes me, as I work with ordinary people from San Diego to Boston to Miami, that those who get involved get results. They don't always get everything they want—nobody does—but they believe there is a fair process and they often win something.

Interestingly, and contrary to the image presented in newspapers and on TV, nearly all of those people who talk to politicians and work with them will tell you that elected officeholders are honest, hardworking men and women of high ethical standards who are trying their best to find satisfactory compromises to complicated problems.

I hope this book will energize you to understand the constitutional role of special interest groups and become engaged and make this democracy work as it should. We don't have political parties that engage citizens to pass legislation. As the founders intended, our system has evolved into a special interest democracy. One of my favorite clients over the years has been realtors. They are fond of saying, "We're not Democrats; we're not Republicans. We are the Realtor Party."

We form and express consensus through myriad organizations, not political parties. That's how advocates gather the critical mass of political weight needed to move Congress or a legislature. It's very important to understand this. When you read in the newspapers or see on TV that the Democratic Party or the Republican Party has done something in Congress or a state legislature, it's misleading. A better description would be "the Democratic caucus" or "some Republicans." To call movers and shakers a "party" invokes an image of citizen participation that simply doesn't exist. We don't enact legislation through parties but through special interest groups. If you doubt this, go down to any party office three months after an election, if you can find one. Try to "join" the party to advocate for your issue. Let me know what happens.

In my seminars I tell people, "All things being equal, politicians will go with the flow. Your job is to create the flow." You can only do that if you represent a consensus rather than a single individual. Usually this means an organization of the sort envisioned in the First Amendment: your association of principals, school board members, food-service workers, superintendents, or parents and teachers. All of these are special interest groups contributing to public discourse and forming public policy.

CONCEPT

All things being equal, politicians will go with the flow. Your job is to create the flow.

HOW TO GET WHAT YOU WANT

The Magic Numbers

It takes 60 votes in the U.S. Senate and 218 in the House to get a bill passed. After that, you need the support of the president and then you have to work with the bureaucrats or regulators. Those people can give you what you want. It's sort of like being in school. You can get 90s and As or you can get 70s and Cs, but you still pass. Anything less than 70 and you fail. When you add 218 in the House and 60 in the Senate, you pass. You win. Anything else is gravy. So these are the magic numbers. (If you face a presidential veto, to override it will take a two-thirds vote in both houses: 67 in the Senate and 290 in the House. Good luck!) In your state legislature, it also takes a magic number. Find out what that number is for your issue and develop your strategy. You can get what you want when you get to that number. For most issues, you can succeed with far fewer, but with those numbers, you can't lose.

Four Essential Tools

1. Professional lobbying staff. You need someone on the inside who understands the system and who will focus on your issues 24/7/365. A volunteer cannot devote the necessary time and can't know enough. Professional staff should help you develop a list of target politicians (who can give you what you want), develop an inside strategy, and tell you what to do and when to do it. The "inside" strategy is the plan to get votes in committee and on the floor and get your bill passed or stopped. The "outside" strategy is how to use money, media, and grassroots advocates in the district to persuade those politicians to vote with you.

2. Money. Anybody who is determined and has something rational to say can get a politician to listen. Just like everyone else, politicians listen best and pay the most attention to people they know and like, who have been supportive. Money demonstrates support. It helps. But plenty of groups win without money, including education groups.

3. Media. Newspapers set the political agenda in their circulation area. Television doesn't. If a newspaper says an issue is important with coverage and editorials, then politicians (and television) will pay attention. Using media to amplify and deliver your message can be a powerful tool. Getting coverage on the editorial pages and in the news pages and on TV can get the attention of politicians whose help you need.

4. Members. As a participant in an organization, your job is to communicate a specific message to the politician in whose district you work or vote. You must convince him or her that (1) a lot of people (2) in the district (3) whom the politician needs (4) care about the issue and (5) care a lot. You accomplish this by describing how the issue affects your life, your work, your schools, your teachers, and your students and by getting others to do the same in a thoughtful, personal manner.

You have enormous power when you tell your personal story, the story of your school, your children, your teachers, your food-service workers, your bus drivers, and the other people who can vote for the person you are talking to. It's almost as strong even if you don't physically live in the district, but work in a school in the district.

Again and again politicians say that they need people like you to help them understand how policy plays out in practice. What is the impact in the classroom? On the teacher? On the learning process? As an educator, of course, you are an expert on this because you live and breathe it every day.

When you realize you only have to talk about the subjects you already know, it makes your job easier. You don't have to be an expert on parliamentary procedure, the committee system, or anything else. You do not need to know how a bill moves through the legislature, although that is useful. Just tell your story.

You come to your elected official as an expert about education and the schools in your area. You know more than they do. You probably know more than the professional lobbyist knows. Your elected officials want to benefit from your knowledge and experience. You can also make the story come alive with personal experiences and specific stories that put a face on the issue and make it memorable.

Your ability to win friends in the legislature or Congress turns more on your ability to make the issue come alive with true stories than any other single factor. Every time I ask a politician to give an example of being influenced, he or she tells about someone who put a face on the issue with a personal story. Like soap opera fans, they love a good story.

1

PEOPLE IN POLITICS

1

The Lobbyists: The Paid Professionals Who Usually Don't Smoke Cigars

In this chapter I offer a few words from people who get paid to make your government work—the professional lobbyists and elected officeholders, as well as their staff members, who can help you get what you want from government.

I start with lobbyists because they are the least understood players to the uninitiated. Lobbyists come to the process both passionately and dispassionately. They all have deep, powerful beliefs about what they do. Many are personally committed to the cause they represent. In many ways they are like lawyers (many are lawyers but by no means all). They are hired to defend a client and succeed on their ability to make the best possible case for that client, regardless of guilt or innocence.

A term lobbyists use to describe themselves time and again is "hired gun." Politicians and staff view them that way too. They often like lobbyists, have close relationships with them, respect them, and trust them. But everyone knows the lobbyist may also be working for the other side a day later, just as a lawyer may work as a prosecutor and then switch to defending criminals. Their message to politicians is always weaker than that of a true believer, a stakeholder, a participant. It's like the defense lawyer who does not say to a judge, "My client is innocent" but rather, "Our position is that he is innocent."

At this writing there are about 35,000 registered lobbyists in Washington competing for time with 535 elected officials and their staff. Someone who has solid experience on a House or Senate committee might be able to leave government and take a lobbying job that starts at $300,000 a year. To retain one of the big lobbying firms might cost an association or corporation $15,000 to $30,000 a month or more, depending on the activity.

3

A continuing theme from all involved in politics is there is a limit to what lobbyists can do no matter how much money they represent and how good the relationship with a politician is. A politician's most important loyalty and dependence is on the voters back home. No politician ever got defeated for making a lobbyist angry, but plenty have been sent packing for making voters angry. That's why your role as a volunteer advocate is so important.

KIMBERLY BARNES-O'CONNOR

This following interview is with Kimberly Barnes-O'Connor, deputy executive director of the national PTA. She is in charge of government relations and lobbying. At the time of this interview, she had been on the job about five months.

Q: Okay, we are talking about PTA and its political activities. What percentage of PTA members would you say are politically engaged enough to write a letter or make a phone call to a politician?

A: 10.

Q: 10%. So you have got 90% upside potential?

A: Absolutely.

Q: What are you going to do to mobilize that other 90%?

A: We are in the process of defining that. Some of it is getting information to them; some of it is training. The most important thing is translating how the skills and abilities that we try to teach them to use on the federal level can be used for local school boards, can be used for state policies, bond issues, whatever is going on. The skills are the same.

Using our member-to-member system, we are trying to help people post messages like "I have this school bond issue on this, this, and this. Has anybody dealt with it?"

The person who writes it may be in Alaska or maybe dealt with it in Montana, or in Vermont. Allowing them to help each other do that. That is the kind of motivation we are trying to achieve. As a national organization we can't get involved in state and local politics. Just because there are too many issues, on things that we see are overarching universal issues we do get involved now.

In building that local and state network of course it will ride on up to federal activity and you have the infrastructure in place. They are most interested in the local stuff. But those same people are the ones that can help federally.

Q: What do you see that you would like to do more or have more of?

A: We have to educate our members, and really it is something we are working on in terms of showing them how things that happen on the federal level transfer down to what happens in their school, and with their kids. That is a hard connection for a lot of people to make. People are really busy with their lives; they want to know, What does that really mean for my kid? What does that really mean for my school? What does that mean for my principal? We have failed to make that connection, so we are working hard on making that connection better for people.

Q: What gets in the way of parents' becoming politically active?

A: They don't see where they come in. It is a matter of whether the time and energy they expend is worth it, whether they can really make change. I think that is a crucial piece.

Q: If you could look every parent right in the eye, what would you say about political action on behalf of kids?

A: I would say they are the biggest group of people who can affect children's lives. That if they can come together on two or three things, not everything, because we are not going to get agreement on everything, but if we can find two or three things that the majority of parents agree with, that we can in fact move mountains. We have 6 million members. We don't mobilize them as well as we could. Part of it is because they don't see the payoff for their time and energy spent.

Q: That is just members; if you expanded to the larger group of parents who aren't members you would have an incredible political force.

A: No question.

Q: What would you like to see parents do? What do you need them to do?

A: I need them to help us identify what issues are topical for them, so that we can get some consensus. We can build some consensus around what are the three big things. Some of that is getting feedback through their local PTAs, through even community boards, any way to get information to the groups. We work with a variety of organizations and agencies, everything from the principals to the elementary school administrators, to superintendents of schools, to school board members, to allied groups.

Q: That goes to identifying issues. What about to increase the clout of parents? To actually move the politicians. What do you need parents to do?

A: I need them to be in contact, to tell legislators what they want. To do so in a concerted way, and in a consistent way. We have a virtual lobbying day here in Washington. Last February we bought in key members of the organization and representatives from key states in terms of their congressional leadership, then had people e-mailing and calling at the same time. That needs to happen not just once a year; it needs to happen consistently over time. Several times a year. You need to build relationships: You need to know who your legislators are, and then feel good about talking to them about what it is that concerns you. I worked on the Hill for twelve years.

Q: Who did you work for?

A: I worked for Nancy Kassebaum and Jim Jeffords. What would move us was when we got letter from parents and kids. I was the children's policy director. I know this one lady, we were working with welfare reform, she was from Kansas, and she said, "It just doesn't pay for me to go to work." She included a breakdown of the money she had when she worked, and she was working a part-time minimum wage job, and then what she got when she was on welfare. She compared the two and included receipts, and included a whole breakdown. There was a $50 difference a month. It was like $47 a month that she lost by going to work.

I was so moved by it that not only did I write the letter for the senator to look at and send, but I called the woman and said, "What do you need? What will help you?" Senator Kassebaum was so impressed she called the lady also and said, "What can we do? What would help? We are in the middle of doing a piece of legislation. Would this help? Would that help? If we changed this? If we changed that?" That was an incredibly powerful response for one woman who just laid out her case very clearly, very simply, said what was important to her. As we worked through the welfare bill the senator would refer back to that letter and say, "Would this help such and such?" This lady became very personal to us.

Q: This is really contrary to the media image of what politicians respond to, which is cigar-smoking lobbyists and money. What was the key element that made the breakthrough here?

A: Because she was somebody who wanted our help. She clearly stated what her problem was, and asked us for help and helped us understand what you go through. Because in all honesty most of the people that work up on the Hill and are elected don't understand what it is like to struggle to get through life, to struggle to get through the month and have enough orange juice by the end of the month or have enough milk or have enough food, and how you parcel that out. It is not a world that people are comfortable with.

Q: Take it back to education. That is good on welfare but if you got a similar story on education of a breakthrough moment of when somebody communicated and made something happen?

A: I can tell you a personal one. I am a parent who has a child in public school. We were negotiating the elementary secondary education bill and I was doing a very small piece of it, but the committee I worked for was doing a very large piece of it. My daughter was in first grade and we had our very first parent–teacher meeting. I asked everybody to take a break so I could go to the meeting and came back.

In the parent–teacher meeting, my daughter is an auditory learner, so I asked them what they were doing to deal with the fact that she is an auditory learner. She certainly is not the only one; it divides to about 50% in any classroom between auditory and visual. They were doing whole language, which was very good for visual learners but very bad for auditory learners. I said what are you doing for the auditory learners. They said, "Well we really can't tailor anything for each individual." I said, "I don't understand. You are a full-time teacher, you have got 22 kids, a reading teacher who is full-time in the classroom, then they have a three-quarter-time assistant teacher, so it seems to me as though you could do something." I said, "If you can't do anything I will get this program [a phonics program], and we will work together. I will just contact you every week and you can tell me what you are working on and I will make sure what I am doing will work on it."

They stood up like they were going to send the phonics police to my house. They were like, "No, don't get that program." I got very irritated. I went back to work right after the meeting. They came to the part of the bill where they started talking about whole language, and they wanted to put some stuff in the bill about whole language and I went ballistic. So the language never went in. That is one thing a parent could do, in my situation. I think that other parents who wrote on education and said, "My kid is in the tenth grade and can't read. Why is that happening? The schools are failing my kid." I think it is because of that outrage that parents thought that if their kids were not succeeding in school, in the reality and the skill basis that they needed, but they kept being passed and passed and passed. What were these kids learning? I think parents got very disgusted with this, and they let people know. We heard from parents all of the time when we were on that bill. We hear from parents here.

We just did a survey of our membership and the number one thing on the minds of PTA parents is student achievement. I don't think they mean student achievement in terms of they are all going to be merit scholars; I think they mean student achievement in terms of "How does my child get the skills and knowledge they need to be successful in life?"

Q: When you were on the Hill what was the volume of communication you got from parents as parents lobbying you compared to professionals in education, principals, superintendents, teachers, people like that? How does that compare?

A: Parents contacted us by letter. We would get several thousand letters a month.

Q: That is a lot.

A: Yeah, it is a lot. From lobbyists we would get maybe one every six months.

Q: I am thinking about the letters from principals back in the district.

A: We don't get them. We rarely get them.

Q: Superintendents and people like that are not communicating in your experience?

A: They use their organization to communicate.

Q: Is that as effective?

A: Not in my mind, and I think not for a lot of professionals on the Hill.

Q: So that is not providing significant and powerful input there?

A: They are sometimes not doing it in a way . . . it is scattered all over the place. It is "I don't like this course," or "I don't like this teacher," or "my school doesn't provide enough recess," or "my school provides too much recess." Schools are difficult in terms of federal legislation because most of the money and most of the power rests at county and state level. The federal government puts in less than 10% of the money. Although the federal policy of No Child Be Left Behind impacts greatly what goes on at state and local level. Again the majority of power is on the state and local level, your local school board, the county board which gives its school board its budget, your state department of education, and governor, that is where most of the decisions are made in terms of what textbooks will be used, in terms of teacher qualifications, in terms of how much authority teachers and principals have.

Q: Well, the same principles apply whether you are talking local, state, federal in terms of how you influence. So one question that often comes up is, You are a lobbyist; what do you need us for? What is it that those parents can do that you can't do? Say to the parents, "I need you to help me" or whatever it is you want to say, what would that be?

A: Your voice is more powerful than the lobbyists. We can go in and make the academic arguments and the research arguments but what really gets people is the anecdotes. What happened to this child? What does my life look like? Unless people get that, they don't make the connection between the research and the policy and what is going on with your child.

Q: When I was in PTA and I had two kids move through public school, it seemed to me that they were really good at raising money and building playgrounds, but the idea of writing a letter or making a phone call never came up. It didn't occur to them. What is going on there?

A: Well, PTA is changing as the times are changing. It is a good thing that it is changing. I keep going to the meetings and saying we are getting into things not only to help their kids, but to help their school and help the world at large. I think as we educate kids, and deal with our education system, that we in fact improve America as a whole, which is one reason why I am here where I am, because I do have that belief. We have volunteer advocates in each state.

Q: Are they professionals?

A: No, they are volunteers within the state PTA organization. We have something called the member-to-member network. The member-to-member network is free. You sign up for it online, then get a weekly posting of what is happening and why in Washington.

Q: All of the politicians, everybody, is for education, and everybody is fighting and we don't seem to be able to make much progress. Why is that? What is going on?

A: Yes, we are all for education; we just don't agree on the road to get there. We agree on the ultimate goal. Some of that breaks down into party politics. Some of it breaks down into geographic regions. Some of it breaks down into theological versus secular. The road to get there has many branches and people keep going down those different branches. I don't think there is a silver bullet. If there was a silver bullet out there to improve education, we could sell it, but we don't have a silver bullet.

Q: You mentioned party politics and one of the things that turns people off and inhibits is what they perceive as conflict and tension. What would you say to parents about the role that you want them to play, to help them understand it isn't that?

A: You have to understand that the media is always looking for a fight, because the story is much better if you have got an argument. Even if you have to find somebody who has no creditability whatsoever, just to get the fight going. But that is what people respond to. It sells newspapers; it gets people looking at news articles and watching broadcast media in a variety of ways. Controversy sells. It is a way also for the media to present both sides of any particular issue.

Q: Tell the parent this isn't what we are talking about. The point that I am trying to make is that legislative lobbying is not campaign politics. Reassure them that this is not what you are asking them to do.

A: No. We don't get into it. We in particular are very nonpartisan. Here is how to find if you are a really good lobbyist. Do the people on Capitol Hill or in the statehouse call you and ask for your opinion? Do they bring you in and ask for information that will help guide their decisions? If you can become that source of information for them, then you have become the most effective lobbyist there is.

It is not about going in and pushing your perspective; it is about becoming a source of information and knowledge that decision makers can rely on. If you have accomplished that, then you have done everything you can. It is building those relationships. Washington, D.C., is a relationship camp. My husband has an old adage which is particularly good for Washington: Friends may come and friends may go, but enemies accumulate.

Nowhere is that more typical than here. I don't go in and try to beat people up, and I don't go in and try to frame things in terms of us or them. If you always focus on your end goal, which is improving the life of kids and families, and improving the education system so that kids can succeed in life and in society, both economically and emotionally, and interpersonally in this world, because school teaches all of that. It is not only academic. You have got to learn to get along with your peers.

Q: I am a parent. I am worried about getting involved in the mud slinging, the controversy, the fight that I see on TV. Help me understand.

A: It's about telling your story, not slinging mud.

MORGAN PLANT

Morgan Plant is a professional lobbyist in Pennsylvania. Her clients tend to be nonprofit organizations that don't have money.

"I get about three calls a day from politicians wanting me to attend fund-raisers. They used to have their secretary call. Now they call in person. It's hard to say no and go in the next day and ask for something.

"I have eleven clients. Most of them don't have much money for contributions. I'll get $100 from this one, $100 from that one, $200 from one, and scrape another $100 from somewhere. That allows me to go to one $500er.

"The [party] caucus fund-raiser tickets are usually $500. Committee chairs cost $350–$500. Leaderships cost $1,000.

"I had a politician speak to a group the other day. He said he spent $500,000 on his last election and he was still in debt $150,000 and that's why money is important. I don't like it that you have to pay to play, but that's the way it is.

"I had 124 cosponsors signed on to a bill this year, a personal best for me. We were up against the doctors. We have a good case. They have a lot of money. Now twenty-eight of the cosponsors have withdrawn."

[*Author's note:* In many states, the way politicians raise money is to throw parties. You pay to go to the party. Maybe it's a dinner, the kind you see on TV that raises hundreds of thousands of dollars. Most are much smaller. One lobbyist told me he had paid $2,500 plus travel expenses from Georgia to go to a breakfast with Senator Joe Lieberman. He got to sit next to the senator and talk about his issue. He felt the money was well spent. Many people have a hard time understanding that a big part of a lobbyist's job is gathering funds from people and buying tickets to parties, dinners, and even breakfasts. But that's one way the business of politics is done.]

TONY DEREZINSKY

Tony Derezinski is lobbyist for the Michigan Association of School Boards. Before becoming a lobbyist, he served as a state senator.

Q: What is that school board members can do that you—a professional lobbyist—can't do?

A: They can help get votes back home. They are constituents and they are also elected officials. They are vote getters in their own right and they can assist or hurt a senator or representative to get votes to get elected.

Q: Are school board members ever seen as potential competition? Is that ever a problem?

A: It's a healthy problem. A number of school board members do run for the legislature. In fact, my member of Congress, Lynn Rivers, got her start on the school board.

Q: Is it a problem that school board members are so enthusiastic about the cause that they think people just ought to be with them automatically?

A: It's something I as a lobbyist work with them on to make sure their message is strong and forthright, factually accurate, and also they see that there are a lot of other issues that take up the time of members of Congress. Their message has to be strong and passionate with the realization that there are other things tugging at the members of Congress and the legislature.

Q: In Michigan you have term limits. What does that do to the grassroots equation?

A: It makes it even more important but it also pushes the process back in time because the window of time these people will be serving is very limited.

[*Author's note:* Michigan legislators are limited to three terms (six years) in the house and two terms (eight years) in the senate.]

It's very important to get to people even while they are just thinking about running to shape their position on issues. They need you more because their time in the legislature is so short. They are just beginning to learn the intricate hoops in education and the state–federal relationship and they need people in the district to tell them the impact of state and federal laws on the district.

Q: What about supporting candidates—engaging in partisan activity? Is there a danger there?

A: They can't do it related to the school board itself, but on their own personal time, sure they can. They should get involved because that's where the real influence is. If in fact they work on their own time for candidates that are favorable toward educational issues then if those candidates get elected they are going to remember them.

Q: How important is it to your success doing your job to have people out working in the districts to support you.

A: Critical. Grass roots is where the power is. I can assist it and I can articulate it in my way in Lansing and Washington. But it's the local constituent who can say, hey, this is how it impacts in your district. Are you going to help or hurt the people in your district on these education issues? They can give the legislator information about what's going on because frequently a legislator's mind isn't made up and he wants to know how legislation impacts back in the district. That comes best from our members who are making decisions on the local school boards. Members in the district are a lot more important than lobbyists. They have the numbers. They have the ability to bring that member of Congress or the state legislature back to the district to meet at the school, to see what's going on.

Q: In the best of all worlds, what would you have school board members do?

A: They would be in continuous contact with the members of Congress and the state legislatures. They would become a source of honest information for that legislator. They would let the legislator know that they are talking to people back in the district about the support or nonsupport they are getting from a legislator. They need to provide the numbers as well. I'm one person. School board members are legion. When I take all the school board members from a senator's district and say we all want to know where you stand and we need you to vote this way, that will be taken into consideration, especially in an election year. You know, read the Medes and the Persians, were you with us or were you against us.

It's especially important during this time in an election year to weigh those legislators in the balance, the Medes or the Persians.

Q: Medes or Persians?

A: That comes from the Bible where they looked at someone very carefully to see whether the came down on the good side or the bad side, to whether they supported education or not. And people should be voting accordingly.

And you need to remember, you can get support most of the time from a good legislator that's on your side, but you also have to give them some slack because they might have some other pulls at the same time.

Q: Do people have to go to the capital to be effective?

A: The power is back in the district. The best work is done back where you live and where your legislator lives. It's much more powerful to have him or her at a local meeting when you confront them and you say these are our issues and these are important. We want your support on this and this. When they are in a local forum and being put on the spot, the pressure is very strong. It may be covered by the media. It will be watched by the people in the room. It's read 'em and weep. Are you evasive? Are you supportive? The power is back home.

Q: I've never heard a politician run against education. They're all for it. So how can you break that apart and make sure you get what you want?

A: As a lobbyist, my job is to convert a vote into something the people back home want. Don't let that bill out of committee. That's what it means to be for education. It's making them realize and not letting there be any deception as to whether a vote is for or against education. You're right, everybody's "for education." But then you get to where the rubber meets the road and that's where I come in. Once people back home understand what's being voted on, they're not going to be fooled by "I'm for education and this vote doesn't hurt you."

Q: I think of a lobbyist as being like a coach, designing the plays and developing the strategy and telling school board members they have to carry the ball.

A: Very good analogy. Coach can't play. He's not a voter in but one district. But these school board members are. They're in the game. It's important for me to be a good coach and make sure people know what's at stake and what's going on. I help them understand the basics of the game. You must be absolutely truthful when dealing with legislators. You never get a second chance if you are dishonest. Be strong. Be passionate. But understand others are equally passionate and want a different outcome. Not to let them off the hook, but to understand the other pressures they are under.

Make sure there is follow-up. When somebody votes with you, let them know you appreciate it. Have an award dinner. Bring them to a meeting and give them some exposure. That will be remembered.

Let them know when they vote against you. They need to know you are watching and will tell them, "This is a vote we do not like and we hope you will be with us on the next one."

Q: Expand on that. Negative feedback is important, but it's easy to get angry and go too far. What are some phrases you might put into a letter or phone call to a legislator who has voted against you?

A: "Dear Senator, we were very disappointed that you voted against a bill we were pushing very hard. It's not done yet since it has to go over to the house and it may get in conference committee, which will give you another opportunity to go along with us. There may also be other legislation that will amend this, so we hope to get support later. We'd like to talk with you about this back in the district, perhaps with other legislators, because this is an issue of crucial importance to us."

Q: What would you think about a letter, "I can't understand how you could vote this way. Can you please explain it to me?"

A: I'd pare that down a little. I'd say, "I'd like to know why you voted the way you did because as I wrote to you, this bill has a very deleterious effect on your district. We're going to be talking about this at our next school board meeting wondering where we are and where we are going."

You cannot get personal and ad hominem because that person will be voting for you or against you on another issue. Stick to the issues. Do not get personal, because all that does is cut off communications and they'll stop listening to you.

Q: Sometimes people pass resolutions from the board and send them in. How would you compare that to individual letters coming in from board members, each letter different?

A: They're both important. For instance, a few years ago we had vouchers on the ballot. We wanted school boards to pass resolutions against school vouchers but we also wanted individual members to write letters. We wanted legislators to know this is something they should go on record as being against.

It was on the ballot, not in the legislature, but we wanted them to go on record against vouchers and about 80% of them did. That included members of Congress. It was defeated 70% to 30%.

Q: What works better, e-mail, phone call, letter?

A: The more personal it is, the more direct it is, the better it is. Face-to-face is best. When you look them in the eye and ask, "Where are you on this issue?" There's tactility there. You're shaking their hand; there's eye contact. The next best would be a phone call, because that's personal and most importantly it should be back in the district. That's where the power is.

Beyond that, it's a letter. When I was a state senator, I kept files of letters on each bill. Every letter I got, I put in a bill file so when I was considering a vote I would have it.

Now we have e-mail. Something more formal like a written letter is more powerful to a politician. But I use e-mail all the time. I have list servers I use so I can get something out to all our members who live in a certain district.

Q: Many times I talk with grassroots advocates and learn they've been communicating with their elected officials and got good feedback. But they didn't tell their lobbyist. When you send out an action alert, how important is it for you to know what people have done, that they have communicated with their legislators?

A: Crucial. Crucial that we know that they follow through and also that we know what response they got. That response then becomes a matter of record. This past year one of the big issues was federal vouchers for the District of Columbia: We don't want them because we think it's the nose of the camel under the tent. We had our members write to the members of Congress to say, "This is bad legislation; don't do it." One member [of Congress] said, "I will only vote for vouchers in the District of Columbia: Never again will I vote for vouchers. I've got a good record on vouchers, but this situation is such that I feel compelled to vote for vouchers for the District of Columbia." That was in writing. Now, when it comes up again, and it will come up again, I have that in writing and his constituents will have that in writing because it was written to a constituent.

So it even works nationally. We can say here's where Representative So-and-so is and, by the way, here is a letter to a local school board member. This is very important. When I send out a blast e-mail, if it's a reasonable number, I will make personal calls to find out what happened. When we go to Washington to meet with members of Congress, we have a form we ask them to fill out right after the meeting so we have a record of what the conversation was about.

Q: Speaking of Washington, a lot of times people go all the way to meet their member of Congress and wind up talking with a staffer. How should school board members feel if they don't get to talk with their representative or senator?

A: It's a very busy place, especially in Washington. Staff has a great hand in shaping the view of that member of Congress. The member may or may not be that tuned in to an education issue. They may not be on the correct committee. It may not be something that was important in their election. But they are interested in it because they are going to be voting on it

A lot of times staff stay. They are constant. They become the experts and if you can influence them, you have a pretty good line on influencing the member. But you do want to meet with the member back in the district when he comes home. You can show them that you have been communicating and you can show them their office has been fully apprised of the issue.

I like to talk with staff people because they know this stuff. Some members of Congress who are on the education and labor workforce committee are very knowledgeable. But some other members of Congress, we can be of great help to them. They frequently call us wanting to know what's the impact back in Michigan.

Q: I'm a school board member from Michigan and go all the way to Washington to sit and explain my issue to some twenty-something kid right out of college. How should I feel about that?

A: You hope they listen. You hope you can shape their views. It's a little disturbing when you realize they've only been on the job a few weeks and you feel you're getting short shrift a little. You want to find out if they are going to be the permanent staffer on education and if so, well, that's where it is. You make it clear you will be following up with the member of Congress to make sure all the views you just expressed are going to get back to him.

You basically have to put pressure on them to make sure your information is getting through. I think to say, "We will be checking to see if this message got through," is fair game.

Q: That sounds a little hardball, a little threatening.

A: It shouldn't be viewed as threatening. It should be viewed as helpful.

Q: Okay. I'm a school board member and I'm a well-known Republican or Democrat and the person I'm talking to, the member of Congress, is of the opposite party. Is that going to work against me?

A: It could, depending on how far you press it. The trick is to say that what you are advocating is good public policy, no matter Republican or Democrat. It's good policy and it's good for the district. A lot of education issues are like that. Both parties will say education is their number one priority.

But then you get to the specifics, and that's where there may be differences. Just stress, "This is how it impacts the district." It has nothing to do with my being a Democrat or a Republican.

Sometimes, frankly, I, having a Democratic background, I have in my private time supported Republicans who have been good to us. If they've helped us, I let people know that.

Q: Some school board members may be ardent Republicans or Democrats and not like people on the other side. What about the idea that as far as education issues go, they have to learn to deal with whoever is in power, regardless of party.

A: Even when the numbers are very even, like here in Michigan where the districts are won or lost by 10,000–15,000 votes, we are a bipartisan state. You focus on the fact that the issues are bigger than the parties. You want to seek agreement. It's achievable. You try to take out the partisan differences and work together. Here in Michigan we have a governor who is a Democrat and a legislature that is Republican.

When I was in the legislature, both houses were controlled by the Democrats and Bill Milliken was a Republican governor. We made a lot of progress. It can be done.

Q: What do superintendents and school boards need to do to empower people like principals to be more effective advocates?

A: A superintendent can have a great impact, both on the board and staff and principals and teachers because they realize the impact legislation has on the running of the schools and on student achievement. That's the empowerment. It's either going to happen to you or you're going to shape what's happening. The people in the house and senate of the legislature and Congress have to hear from you. Board members don't have the technical knowledge that a superintendent or principal has. They can say, this is how the issue affects my building, and that in turn empowers the school board member to say, hey, we feel trapped because this is going to affect us negatively.

It's very important to be advocates because it will make a difference. If you just stand by, it will be done unto you. But teachers, school board members, principals all have their own associations. Work with your association. Get more information. Get involved. Build a relationship with your senator and your representative and their staff. Bring that legislator back into your school so people can find out where they stand. Not in a hostile way. But in a very direct, forward way. When they vote your way, be happy. If they don't have a vote yet, give them the information that will make their minds up.

When they don't vote your way, let them know you are aware of it. When they are back in the district, ask them about it.

Believe you can have an influence of public policy. That's the most important thing of all.

Q: How important are the stories and anecdotes people tell?

A: The more the better. Right now we are working on a project for No Child Left Behind, this massive and underfunded federal law. We are working with school superintendents in the districts of selected members of Congress who are on education and the workforce (committees) to help them understand what specific provisions of the law are going to cost.

We went to Washington a month ago to talk about problems with No Child Left Behind like trying to test children with limited proficiency in English. We object to that because they don't understand the language of the test. How in the world are they going to be scored fairly on that? Now the U.S. Department of Education is backing off that and coming up with an alternative time frame and an alternative method to test those children. There's an example of where pressure worked.

BARRY SACKIN

Barry Sackin was a school food-service director for 14 years. Now he is vice president of policy for the American Food Service Association.

Q: Why do you need your members to lobby?

A: The reality is that our members are the experts. The goal is for practitioners to talk with legislators and their staffs. In the U.S. House this year there will be about 4,000 bills introduced. There's no way members of the House and their staff can understand all those issues and topics and so they turn to experts. The experts in this case are the people who day in and day out serve children. Our members are not only the experts; they are the constituents, the ones who vote. We're here in Washington and yes, we know a lot about the issues and we have relationships, but I don't vote in the district in Arizona. Our people out there are more convincing than we are.

Q: Many people like your members are intimidated by the process. They think they have to understand about legislation and the process. What does a politician want from a volunteer advocate?

A: We in Washington get paid to understand the legislative process. We help our members understand what needs to be done and when. Members of Congress and their staff understand the legislative process. What members of Congress need is information about the programs. That can only come from people who do it every day.

Q: You can put on the table all the data and statistics about what children are eating or whatever. What does the volunteer need to bring to the table?

A: What our members bring are the stories. We are in the midst of what could be a very big legislative success having to do with raising eligibility for school meals. Part of that success is because 500 local school boards around the country have passed a resolution telling Congress they should do this. Those boards got their information from our members who understand the issue.

When our members write to Congress we ask them to include those personal stories. So on March 12 the Senate adopted a budget resolution that includes taking the first step in what we call eliminating reduced price. Senator Elizabeth Dole of North Carolina introduced the amendment to provide the funding, and included in her presentation to the full Senate was our list of state and local school boards that support it. She told two stories from constituents back in North Carolina who spoke with passion about the difficulty children have getting 40 cents to pay for lunch. It doesn't seem like a lot of money but to those kids, it is.

It's those personal stories, those heartfelt stories, that our members bring that help members of Congress understand the impact of legislation they're considering.

Janey Thornton in Kentucky is the state legislative chair and incoming president. Virtually every county in Kentucky has passed this resolution and it's because of her grassroots efforts. I think that's over 80 counties in Kentucky.

Q: It sounds like a great deal flowed from the efforts of one very committed person.

A: It's an amazing thing. You need a champion. In the Senate, the champion was Elizabeth Dole. Her maiden speech in the Senate talked about hunger and how it agonizes her and how she became committed to do something about it. In Kentucky, Janey was the champion. She adopted this and she put her energy into it. It is amazing what a difference it makes when one individual is willing to put in the time to bring others along.

Q: I wonder if school boards understand the importance of this kind of activity, if they realize how much impact they could have if they would empower those people downstream in the school system to become advocates. Is it ever a problem that school boards are restrictive about people becoming political advocates?

A: The concept of advocacy is something they are familiar with. They are lobbied all the time. We work very closely with the school board association and they are rather envious of our success at the moment. Some school boards, because they say it's public dollars, are more restrictive than others. In our efforts we talk to school boards but we also talk to PTAs and nurses and we work in large coalitions.

There's another message that goes along with the idea of school boards empowering people, and that is that your voice is much more powerful when you work in a coalition of like-minded people. Everyone expects school food-service people to pass the resolution we've asked for. But a resolution from a school board is a very powerful message.

Q: People think they are too busy and don't have time to become an advocate. What does it take?

A: Becoming a volunteer advocate can be a very simple thing or can be a very intense activity depending on the level of interest. Yesterday we sent out a blast e-mail to 15,000 ASFS members with a simple message: Fax your member of Congress saying when the budget resolution comes up they need to include our initiative. It's nothing more than send a fax. Our website has a fabulous section where members can just type in their zip code and send an e-mail to their representative. It can be that simple.

Q: According to the Congressional Management Foundation, members of the House—the House alone—are expected to get 130 million e-mails. Are they effective?

A: It's an interesting question whether e-mails are an effective way of communicating with your representative. A number of years ago I was in a presentation that said members of Congress know that every letter they receive represents 10,000 opinions of people who didn't write. They would literally take the yes letters and the no letters and stack them up and see which pile was higher. I suspect they keep some similar tally of e-mails.

I was in a senator's office and there was a hot issue on the floor and there was a receptionist who was doing nothing but answering the phone and saying, "How do you want him to vote?" and keeping the tally.

At a minimum, it works that way. We are asking in the current campaign that they fax because it creates a piece of paper that has to be handled, reviewed, and read. So it depends on the issue and the timing. We used to encourage letters. Unfortunately, with all the security in place now, letters may take weeks to get through. A fax or e-mail must be responded to immediately. E-mail? I haven't seen any data on how Congress is weighing e-mail. It's so easy. But last year we used e-mail on a budget issue that would have done harm to us and we generated 15,000 e-mails in two weeks. We were successful, so we think that had some effect.

Q: Do you ask people to send in targeted e-mail to key decision makers in Congress or do you ask everybody to e-mail everybody?

A: Every situation is different. There is no pat answer. Our efforts right now focus on the House Budget Committee. We are asking our members to contact their representative—that's *their* representative. Now if the budget committee members receive letters from 250 or so members of Congress, they are marking up the budget on Wednesday and we'd like them to have sense for where their constituents are or where their colleagues are on our issue.

Q: I'm hearing a two-tiered effort. You are trying to get Dear Colleague letters and constituent letters to the members of the decision-making committee. If you read the newspapers and watch TV, you might think that Congress only responds to people who make campaign contributions. You are not a group that's ever going to use money as a tool. How does that affect your ability to influence Congress?

A: It's very interesting the concept that money and PAC contributions have on influence. We have a very small PAC. We call it a thank-you PAC. We only give to people who are in Congress who have demonstrated support for our programs. We certainly don't have enough money to influence anybody's vote. But it has been effective in getting us an opportunity to present our case.

We are what is generally known as a "white hat" group. We're doing things for kids. Marshall Max, our legislative counsel, had an opportunity to talk with an influential senator. After he made his pitch for child nutrition, the senator said, "Of all the people in this room, all these people are trying to get something for their client so their client could make money or something. You're here doing something for kids." What we're advocating for isn't a special interest; it's for the general good.

The transportation bill is always a big deal when it comes up. Every member of Congress has a transportation project. They all want to go home and campaign, "I brought this much money into the district to invest in our community and our infrastructure."

What our members are coming to understand is that every member of Congress has schools in their district. All those schools have food-service programs. Therefore as a constituent service doing things for that group is a good thing. It's not influence in terms of campaign contributions; it's that there are a lot of kids who have a lot of parents; a lot of whom vote. They want to be responsive to that constituency.

Q: What is the importance of getting to know members of Congress and their staff and being known compared to just sending in e-mail and letters?

A: I get really excited when one of our members calls me and says, "Senator

So-and-so's staff just called me and this issue is coming up and they want to know what my opinion is." I know we have been successful and our members have been successful when that member of Congress looks to us to understand an issue.

Just last week on the House Education and Workforce Committee a congresswoman from New York was in an e-mail exchange almost every fifteen minutes with one of our members in New York about an issue that was being discussed. That's a mark of success, when our member becomes the resource.

Q: What do people need to do to build a relationship so they get the phone call from a legislator?

A: It's just as important to build relationships with staff as it is with members of Congress and it's the same as any other relationship. Introduce yourself. Make yourself available. Communicate not just when you need something, but just checking in from time to time. Members of Congress have lots of people doing that. The challenge with staff is the turnover. You build a relationship and then they leave and you have to start over again. But hopefully that person keeps their contact list and when the issue of child nutrition comes up again, your name is there. It takes time, but it's worth the effort.

Q: The staff in Washington is often very young and inexperienced, maybe on their first job. How can people deal with that?

A: First, they *are* congressional staff. They talk to either the member of Congress or the staff director. At a markup of the Education and Workforce Committee last week, there was a roll call vote. Well, those members had not been present during the debate and they had to depend on their staffers to tell them how to vote. There's no question that staff is key. When I was a school food-service director and coming to Washington as a grassroots advocate, I would be talking face-to-face with a member of Congress with the staffer behind them and that staffer is the one I'm focused on educating. That's reality.

Q: People worry that I'm a Democrat and the member of Congress is a Republican or vice versa: How important is that?

A: Child nutrition is a nonpartisan issue. We're talking about feeding kids. So I don't think it's important at all. Of course, you're going to take advantage of whatever biases are important to understand the member of Congress. What their issues are and their approach and try to make your arguments fit within their philosophical outlook.

About seven or eight years ago I went to see a congressman, who has since retired in California. I had a relationship because his district overlapped my school district and I had a colleague with me. So the two of us went in.

My political stripe was very opposite to this member of Congress. My colleague obviously had an opposite political stripe, and the member of Congress laughed and looked at me and said, "Well, we'll educate this guy." He had no idea I was politically different than he was.

When I went in, I talked about child nutrition. I always presented the issue in ways that were consistent with his philosophy.

Q: Sometimes people come to Congress and they have this laundry list of five or ten things they want to talk about. What's your recommendation for the number of issues to bring up in a meeting?

A: It's important to be very narrow and very focused. As a citizen, I have lots of things that concern me. When I talk to a member of Congress, I only talk about one thing. In terms of the ask, there are a couple of things that are important. Have no more than three things you want and preferably just one. Never leave an office without asking for a specific action. Hold them responsible for it. If you ask them to cosponsor bill XYZ and they say, "Yes we will," then a week later if you go on the web and don't see any action, you have to call and say, "When I met with the congressman last week, he said he was going to cosponsor this and I don't see his name on the list."

If the request is to write a letter, say I want a copy of the letter. In our case, we want letters to Chairman Russell on the House Budget Committee. So if someone says, "I will write that letter," then I say, "Can I get a copy so I can share with our members back home to let them know you are standing up for us?" Always have a specific ask, as narrow as possible; you don't want them to do everything under the sun, just this one little thing.

Hold them responsible. Do the follow-up. Always be courteous. Always say, "Thank you." But hold them responsible.

Q: What about these folders of information, these leave behinds that everyone has with pages and pages of issues and information. Does anyone ever read it?

A: We do a legislative issue paper as part of our legislative conference each year. In the past two years because we are in the middle of child nutrition reauthorization, we've had a fairly long list. When some of our people went in the staffer had read the documents. They were really prepared.

And to touch back on something we mentioned before, when people come to Washington, they want to meet with their member of Congress. The reality is the work is being done by the staff. There's nothing wrong with not meeting with a member of Congress but meeting with a staffer. Some of our members come back from the Hill and they will say, "I talked with the staff and the member stopped in to say hello." That's wonderful. They had their chance for the handshake photo op, but they also got the work done.

Q: How would you compare lobbying and advocacy done back home to what you do here in Washington?

A: It's really important for people to understand that the Constitution of the United States gives us the right to petition Congress. It is our right and it is our responsibility. What we do here in Washington, those of us who are hired to advocate, is talk to the committees that do the work, explaining the details to the people who are writing the bills. My effectiveness comes from the fact that I'm speaking for 55,000 members back home. So we have a fair amount of input into what is in a bill. That doesn't necessarily translate into influence, but we have input.

It is the people back home who are voters who affect how a member of Congress is going to decide an issue. Some groups have strictly the grassroots element, but they don't have the time—they're all working—to do the kind of in-depth policy work we do here. So you need both, professionals working here, people working back at home.

Q: Does a person have to come to Washington to lobby in order to be effective?

A: It is not essential and sometimes what you do back home is better. We have encouraged our people to contact the local office, which tends to focus on constituent services and casework, not policy work, and build relationships with them as well as the policy people here in Washington.

The most effective thing we do is have our members invite members of Congress into the school to have lunch with the kids. If you want to get a member of Congress really listening to you and spending time with you, give him an opportunity in an election year to have his picture taken with a kid eating lunch sitting on those little chairs at those little tables listening intently to a child. It is an opportunity for them to see and experience what you do and for you to talk with them in the setting you are most comfortable with. As a by-product, they may get on the front page of the newspaper.

Those relationships back home, getting them to hit the ground—we all read about those congressional delegations that go to Iraq to see the war on the ground—well, for us, the ground is in the school cafeteria. Maybe on the ground for transportation is a construction site. Those visits are as important as what people do here in Washington. On the other hand, we had a thousand people here two weeks ago. We had buttons that said ERP—eliminate reduced price—which is our highest agenda right now. You want to get somebody's attention? Have a thousand people wearing a button they don't understand and you have to ask what's it all about. People start to pay attention.

It's rare that I'm up on the Hill and I don't see a bunch of veterans in their hats or somebody else wearing buttons and going from office to office. You see them and you want to know what their issues are.

Q: What about talking to a member of Congress if I'm not from their district?

A: If you are not from their district, they may or may not listen or pay attention. There are 435 members of the House and when we have our legislative day, we do not have a person from every district. In that case, it's helpful to have someone from the district make the appointment for you. Then you can say, "I'm here for Suzy from the district who couldn't be here and she asked me to share her views." But they really want constituents. The first thing you will usually be asked when you call a congressional office is "What's your zip code?" They want to know if you are a constituent. It does make a difference. They are so busy.

There are people in this country who look at the salaries of members of Congress and say, "These people get paid too much. Look at how much more they make than the rest of us." But those members of Congress and their staff work incredibly hard. And their first job is to get elected again. And so they are going to pay attention to the voters back home. It's not unreasonable for them to not be able to talk to people they don't represent.

Q: In a big state like California, New York, or Florida, how can a person get to see and know and be recognized by a senator?

A: In some states like Delaware, Vermont, or North Dakota, you may actually have a better chance of meeting a senator than a representative. Senators have larger staffs than House members and so it should not be too difficult to meet with a staffer. Senator Boxer or Feinstein from California has 35 million constituents and they don't have any more hours in the day than a senator from Montana. It's not likely they will be able to meet with everyone who wants to meet with them.

What you do over time is build a relationship with staff so when you finally need to meet with the senator, you get the meeting. But in the senate, staff is even more important.

Q: What do you need members to do to achieve the association's political goals?

A: Build your comfort and confidence in your role as a lobbyist. "Lobbyist" is not a four-letter word. You are the expert. Your job is to build relationships and credibility with members of Congress and their staff.

When a member of Congress says, "I'm going to do something for kids because it's the right thing to do," and you know you have helped him make that decision, there are very few things as rewarding as having that sense of making a difference.

STEVE DEWITT

Steve DeWitt is associate director of government relations for the National Association of Secondary School Principals.

Q: You are the professional lobbyist. Why do you need your principals to communicate with members of Congress?

A: The member of Congress is not going to listen to me as much as someone from the district. They are the voters. They provide the money for the campaigns. That's who the senators and representatives serve.

In order for me to do my job, the constituent back home has to back up what I'm saying. The member of Congress has to know I'm reflecting what the people back home want. Our principals are the connection that we need. They are the people the senators and representatives at the federal and state level listen to. They can personalize the message.

Q: What is it like when you go in to talk with a member of Congress and they have not heard from your principals?

A: It's hard to get them interested. If I go to an office and they have received no letter or phone call from the district, they are not going to care about the issue.

Q: What if they have received some letters and phone calls?

A: They listen much more readily. Each member is dealing with multiple issues so it's sometimes difficult to get in, but that's why we need more contact from principals back home so we get our issue noticed.

We're currently dealing with No Child Left Behind. Our state president from Alaska has had a very good contact with Senator Murkowski. She has contacted us about making some improvements in the law. That would not have come about without our principal in Alaska talking to the senator. She's hearing that the law is having an effect in her state and she's come to us.

Q: Many people in the country would be very suspicious, even cynical about that statement. They read about the "Beltway mentality" and how Congress is isolated from the people and doesn't care about them.

A: They have to care. Those are the people that voted them into office and can vote them out. Whether you are a member of Congress who likes that fact or not, you have to deal with it. Certainly when it comes to the technical aspects of how to get a bill passed, a principal may not be the best person to answer questions, but principals are the best ones to explain how legislation affects schools.

Q: When principals speak with a member of Congress, what do they need to do to get their attention, to be remembered?

A: When we bring our principals here to lobby, we advise them to have stories from back home that illustrate what they are dealing with, a personal story about a specific student in a specific school and what's happening to him or her. Instead of using that inside-the-Beltway language, you need to personalize the issue.

A lot of principals are fearful of getting involved thinking they have to do more than that. You just need to tell the story of what's happening in your school and leave it to the legislator to figure out why the law needs to be changed this way or that way. A good legislator can do that.

Q: People are often disappointed when they come all the way to Washington and talk to a twenty-something staffer. How should they feel about that?

A: It may be more important to get to know the staffer because in a lot of offices, the staffer does all the legwork on an issue. In some cases the staffer may brief them on an issue they know nothing about and the member of Congress will take their opinion. Even though people are in their twenties, it's amazing how much responsibility they have. You should not be disappointed and should follow up with those staff people when you get home. Invite them to your school. Form a relationship with that staffer as much as the congressperson.

Q: When a principal talks to one of these young people on the Hill, it may feel like he or she is talking to a student. Do they need to change their approach in any particular way?

A: You certainly don't want to talk down to them. Deal with them just as you would want to be dealt with on a professional level. Talk to them as though you were speaking to a member of Congress because in many ways, you are. There's no need to change the way you are as an individual; just treat them with mutual respect.

If your style is to come in and present a lot of statistical information, that's great. If you don't have that, don't worry about it. Speak from your knowledge and experience, with respect.

Q: Let me challenge you. Given the choice between presenting a lot of statistics and data and a story about a kid in a school, which would you go with?

A: The best-case scenario would be both. Tell the story and then back it up with the statistical information. Information has become very important. Everything needs to be research based. Everything needs documentation. If you don't have the data, go back to your association lobbyist. Come to me and say the staff person asked for this or that. That's our job, to get back with the information.

Q: Do you ever see situations in which Congress is faced with dueling data? You have information, the other side has information, and the decision will be a political one anyway, so what does the data matter?

A: It does happen. There are good and bad points to both sides. But you have to be able to neutralize the other side. It often comes down to building a network of individuals back home who can back up what you're saying. That's why it's important for principals to get others involved, teachers, parents, friends, and others in the community.

In the past principals have been hesitant to be active on political issues, but the landscape has changed, especially since the passage of laws like No Child Left Behind. More principals now understand that if they don't get involved, someone is going to get involved for them and pass legislation they aren't going to like.

Q: It's important for principals to get involved politically, but they have a school board to deal with, a superintendent, how do they get around that?

A: Sometimes that's an issue. If your superintendent tells you not to lobby, you don't lobby. But there are other ways to inform your congressperson. You have to weigh the pros and cons of getting involved, but I don't see a lot of superintendents stepping in and saying, "Don't do that," or school boards, although it does happen.

Q: In an ideal world, what would be the message from school boards and superintendents to principals about advocacy?

A: To communicate to legislators at the state and federal level what the needs are in your school. To put it in terms of the needs of your students.

Q: School boards and superintendents would be better off if they encouraged and enabled everybody downstream to advocate for schools.

A: Right.

Q: Principals don't have much spare time to take on another list of to-dos. What does it take to be effective?

A: It doesn't take much time to send an e-mail to your congressperson. Our association has instituted a legislative action center online that helps principals identify their congressperson and their staff. That's very easy to use. If you set aside once a week to take five minutes to read our website and send a message about what's going on.

Q: In the House alone this year there are predictions of 130 million e-mails. What can a principal do to make sure anyone even sees that e-mail?

A: Follow up with a phone call. This goes to the different levels of participation and effectiveness. Start with an e-mail. Next, try to build a connection, a relationship so it's easy to pick up the phone, call, and they know you have information they want and need.

Just call your congressperson's office and ask who handles education issues. It's usually the legislative assistant, but it may be someone else. The most powerful person in an office in terms of policy is probably the administrative assistant or the chief of staff or the legislative director.

Q: Can you think of a good example of a principal doing what we want him to do and getting a good result?

A: Yes. We have a principal in Utah who used the legislative action center to send an e-mail to his congressperson and got an immediate answer back and from that has built a good connection with the office.

A member of Congress is much more likely to call someone they know, and so if you get in there enough times so they know you, they will depend on you as a resource.

Q: You don't have a PAC. What do your principals need to do, if anything, to compensate for that and to use money as a tool of advocacy?

A: Money is important. But members of Congress tend to see our principals as leaders in the community and they depend on the leaders to advise them. That counterbalances the money issue to some extent. You have to work with what you have. You can also get other principals and other people involved in carrying the message.

Q: Should principals make individual contributions?

A: It's helpful. It varies from office to office as to how people view campaign contributions. It probably helps you get access.

Q: How important is it to go to Washington compared to what you do back home in the district?

A: Washington visits are important. They reinforce what you've been doing all year. It shows the members of Congress you care enough to come here. You're watching what they do. To have a lot of principals here on one day makes a statement.

Q: What is the appropriate language to use when you aren't happy with your member of Congress?

A: Certainly you want to remain respectful. You don't want to be yelling at them. "Disappointed" is a good word. Convey why you are disappointed and what the effect is on your school. Let them know you aren't going to just accept what they are doing; you're going to talk with other people in the community and let them know as well.

Sometimes in the rush of things here Congress people aren't as informed as they should be. When you let them know, they may change their mind.

Q: Every politician is for education. So why do we have to fight so hard to get what education needs?

A: Everybody is on the bandwagon for education. But when you get down to the specifics, that's when you see who the education supporters are and are not. It's important for principals and lobbyists to question the decisions that are being made, to ask each member of Congress, "Why did you make that decision?" To ferret out what their support for education really is.

Many people say they support education, but when you look at the votes or see how much money is going to education, you see a very different story.

Q: Principals and school board members do what they do because they are passionate about it. But passion is not enough, right?

A: If you can maintain your passion and let people know that you are motivated to do good for your students or your school, that's the thing. We talked about data earlier. It's important to balance your passion with good reason, to show the school is using its money effectively. Educators are often accused of always asking for money. If you can connect the dots and show what the federal funding is doing, that's key. But be passionate as well. Show your passion but control your emotion.

Q: Getting to a senator in a large state is terribly difficult. What advice do you have to help penetrate the palace guard and talk to their U.S. senator?

A: Start with staff. If you have anything special or different in your school, highlight that. If you have an event, Congress members are always interested in a good photo op that will demonstrate they are supporters of education. Find out when they are going to be in the state and invite them over. They are much more accessible when they are in the state than when they are in Washington. Be persistent. Don't give up. It is difficult.

Q: As we speak, we're heading into the election season. What do principals need to do to take advantage of the election cycle?

A: The months preceding an election are prime time to invite them to your school for an event, a photo op. If you've had a problem, telling people about it and getting them to mention it to the candidates can be powerful. When they're looking for votes they may decide to address some of your issues.

Q: If I tell my member of Congress I'm going to inform, say, parents and others of a vote I thought was wrong, they are going to perceive that as a threat.

A: You want to be respectful, but you can point out a negative consequence. As long as you are shedding light on an issue as opposed to a personal attack on the congressperson you should be okay. You can say, "Congress needs to address this," in a broader way and get out of the political side of it.

Q: What would you like to say to every principal?

A: Your voice counts. You can make a difference. But to make a difference, you have to get your message to the congressperson or staffer. A few years ago we would quite often get a member of Congress who would say, "I just don't hear from principals. I want to hear from principals, but I don't."

I would have to reach out to principals to get information. That tells me a lot of our members aren't expressing what's on their mind. Hopefully that's changing.

I'd like to say to principals that you yourself may be a good advocate and we need to get others involved as well. Maybe the principal down the street isn't engaged and needs a little motivation, a little encouragement, a little mentoring to get involved.

Don't be intimidated by the process in Washington. We're currently in the budget cycle, preceded by the president's budget, then the appropriations cycle, the authorization cycle . . . it can be confusing. So just stick to what you know as principals. Talk about your experience and knowledge. That's all you need to do.

Use local media. That's an important part of advocacy that people don't think about. Sending a letter to the editor is a great way to get a legislator's attention, whether state or federal. Believe me, they are going to see that and react. Most of the offices in Congress have people who go through those papers every day and they cut out those stories and letters and editorials.

Many times a principal is used to dealing with the local newspaper and TV people and hasn't thought about using that contact to have an impact on politicians. You can pick up the phone to local media just as easily as to the member of Congress.

MICHELLE WHITE

Michelle White is spokesperson and advocacy manager for the National Association of Secondary School Principals.

Q: You used to be a staffer in Congress.

A: I worked for Senator Jeff Bingaman.

Q: You were one of those twenty-something staffers who make Congress work. A lot of people who come to Washington for the first time are surprised and disappointed. They expect to meet with the member of Congress and wind up talking to someone who reminds them of their son or daughter.

A: I have heard this often from our members. It is perhaps a little off putting to sit across the table from somebody who looks like me. You have to keep in mind that these people have personal interaction with the representative or senator. Often the opinion they form of you and your cause carries tremendous weight with the member of Congress. You should treat them as an equal. Often these people are right out of school and don't know much. You should as clearly and simply as possible explain the issue and why it's important. Explain Title 1 to them in concrete ways they can understand.

Q: In fact there is a lot of turnover in these staff positions and you may come to Washington three years in a row and have to educate someone from zero each time.

A: That's part of the process. A lot of folks are surprised at how young Capitol Hill is. There are many reasons for that, but it doesn't diminish the importance of getting them to understand the needs of schools and students and administrators.

Q: People come to Washington, put on their name tags, and go from office to office leaving these vast files of information. What happens to that stuff?

A: If it's hard to get through, it's not going to be got through. It will end up in the trash. If it's crisp, clear, and easy to read, it will get filed, maybe looked at and filed away. The most important thing is to make a compelling case in person. Leaving materials has its place. It serves as a refresher for staff so they can get the high points. If it's not a clear, talking-points format, it's not going to be read.

Q: I've heard that nobody on Capitol Hill will read anything longer than one page; maybe we should just leave one page.

A: [Smiling and nodding yes] It wouldn't hurt to leave just one page. If it takes two pages, that's fine. But don't stretch it out to ten pages to impress them because that defeats your purpose.

Q: Some members of Congress aren't on the committee of jurisdiction for your issues and won't get involved in the details. What do they need?

A: It's always important that members of Congress hear real-life stories, something they can take to their colleagues. If they don't happen to be on the Education Committee, then obviously they don't have a vote when your issue is in committee. But they may have a friend who is on the committee and they may vote when it comes up on the floor. So if they have a concrete example of how this money or that regulation affects constituents in their district it's going to help you case tremendously.

Q: Obviously with so many people coming in every day, not everything is passed on to the senator or representative. How much gets passed on?

A: That will vary from office to office and depends some on the level of staffer you are talking to. If you are talking to a legislative correspondent, your odds aren't as high as if you are talking to a legislative assistant. It depends on how important the issue is to them. In a good office, probably 70% is passed on. But each office is different.

Each office is its own small business and that's important to understand. Just because they are in the same building doesn't mean they are all connected.

Q: I once took a group in and they were turned over to, and this was the title on her card, the "junior legislative assistant." If you are turned over to someone like that, what does that mean?

A: It could mean the higher assistant is in a meeting and couldn't get away and would have loved to talk with you. It could be a sign you aren't important to them and so they gave you the low man on the totem pole. But you don't want to leave a bad impression with that individual. If you sell your points to them, they will be impressed with you and say to their boss, "I had an amazing experience with this person and we should take a careful look at what they are saying."

The best thing you can do is make friends with somebody in an office like that. When they go into a meeting with another office or a member of Congress, you're in the back of their mind when your issue comes up.

Capitol Hill is a fascinating place. It's about who you know. A junior staffer in the Senate becomes a senior staffer on the House side. If you've made your points with that junior staffer in the Senate, you're going to have a champion in a senior position in the House. After a few years perhaps that person goes to a committee. From the committee work they go back to the Senate. Then you have someone who is pretty well established on the Hill and in that committee. It's somebody you started with four or five years back who is now well versed on your issue and they want to see you do well.

So even if you are meeting with the most junior person, you should take full advantage of it because you're in the door with somebody who can help you.

Q: How many thank-you notes did you get when you were working on the Hill?

A: Not nearly enough. A lot of people underestimate the value of a thank-you note. It's a good way to remind them of what you talked about. Show them you really were grateful but also "In the meeting we talked about . . ." That serves as a reminder that meeting meant a lot to me and it helps them remember what you talked about.

Q: Is it possible to communicate too much, to become an irritant?

A: It depends on the message. If you are sending sincere messages about what's happening in your school, and this is what we need, that's legitimate. You're keeping them informed.

If the messages aren't focused, you're not asking for anything, there's no coherent message, it can be tiresome and leave a bad impression.

Q: Did you ever get people coming in angry? How do staffers respond to that?

A: There's upset and passionate and there's irrational anger. There are plenty of things that happen in Washington, D.C., that do not translate well on the local level. People have a right to be upset and staffers need to hear when things aren't working. But if someone goes into an office and is irrational and makes a personal attack against a staffer or member, it definitely creates a negative impression.

Q: People come in wearing these little badges "I vote." The implication is that if you're not with me, my vote and your election are at risk.

A: That's the biggest thing you have. As a constituent, you vote that member in and out of office. It's important to remind these folks of that. When they realize that not only did you come to Washington with your concerns but also you vote and you can influence the vote of others, it's a very powerful tool. Principals as leaders in the community will have the ear of the community, the parents, all those folks. Principals should exercise that power.

Q: I have heard some staffers say those badges, "I vote," feel a little like a threat. If you don't do what we want, we'll vote against you. People also come and say, "You work for me." Does that work?

A: It's a fine line. You have to be evenhanded and realize that staffers and members make hundreds of decisions every day. It's important to make your case without being threatening per se. It doesn't help to say, "I'm not going to vote for you if you don't see things my way." That doesn't go over well.

Just wearing a sticker that says, "I vote," is a good reminder that you do vote in the community and your opinion matters at the poll.

Q: If you could speak to each of your principals about advocacy, what would you say?

A: Members of Congress don't hear from principals enough. In this day and age when the federal government is coming into the classroom, you must make your voice heard. It's not an arduous process. It's not complicated. It doesn't take hours a day just to write a letter. We work very hard to make it easy for principals to communicate with Congress. A phone call can make a world of difference.

A lot of folks are cynical that it won't matter. One letter from this principal in town A and he tells another principal, maybe that letter will snowball into twenty letters and that makes a huge difference.

When I was on the Hill, I saw letters all the time from teachers and from parents. I never saw one letter from a principal. I was handling education and it would have mattered a lot if I had just seen one letter from a principal. Unfortunately, I never received that one letter.

NANCY STANLEY

Nancy Stanley was associate executive director of the Michigan Association of School Administrators, where she managed and implemented legislative services for Michigan's school administrators, working with state government officials and local school superintendents to support legislation benefiting students. She is a former teacher and has also served as a policy analyst for the Michigan House of Representatives.

Q: To what extent is it possible and desirable to mobilize your members?

A: It's highly desirable, both for the lobbyists and the association. Legislators listen to the grassroots people more readily than the lobbyists. They know the lobbyists have a vested interest in promoting their agenda. And the lobbyists usually can't vote for the legislators. When the grassroots people come in, that equates to votes. They are constituents.

Q: If an administrator who lives in Lansing communicates with a legislator who lives in Grand Rapids—in other words, they are not a constituent—how effective is that?

A: If the legislator has a power position, say, the speaker or majority leader or chair of the Education Committee, it has more of an impact. If you are from Lansing and the legislator from Grand Rapids is a friend and you have a relationship, that has an impact.

Q: To what extent would you like to see superintendents empower other people to write letters?

A: That's very helpful. We're having difficulty getting superintendents to write letters. If we can get them to and then get others to as well, that's very powerful and very helpful to us. Recently the management lobbyists have started working with the union lobbyists, and on those issues where we have similar concerns, using teachers, administrators, and all the people in between is very powerful.

Q: I want to dwell on this issue of superintendents empowering others because I think they may be reluctant, perhaps worried that people might become loose cannons and cause problems. Why is it important that superintendents empower others and get them to write letters and make phone calls?

A: Once a legislator understands that a superintendent is speaking for a number of people in the district, that's powerful. Second, just sheer numbers of e-mails, letters, and phone calls count. I don't think the general public understands how much impact you can have with one letter or one phone call. They think legislators get a lot of phone calls and letters, and they do, but not on the same subject and not always from their constituents. So while they may get a hundred letters in a day, but they might be on a hundred different topics. So if you empower others to write and suddenly they get ten letters from constituents . . . it gets their attention.

Q: Wouldn't you also say that people with technical expertise in senior positions who live in the district and are talking about the legislator's schools and kids bring something additional to the table.

A: Absolutely. Recently our speaker had a computer issue. He wanted to get computers in the classroom. Having a technical person talk with him about how this was wise or not wise had a great deal of impact. More than having the superintendent call and say I like this or I don't.

Q: Then there is also the political component, right, having people talking out there in my district where I have to run again. Pretend I'm an administrator. Persuade me I can make a difference.

A: I've been trying to do that. It is difficult to do. You have to get a positive experience or get a colleague to talk with them. Someone has to go in and say, "I went in and talked to Representative So-and-so and he's going to support our position. You need to talk with your representative because we need that vote as well." As superintendents have success and talk with other superintendents, that's more helpful than anything I can do.

Q: What about school boards? Do they make it clear that this is part of a superintendent's job and encourage the superintendent to engage in advocacy?

A: It depends. You have some that are pretty active and you have some that would prefer their superintendents not get involved in issues.

Q: In terms of your job, what would be the ideal situation?

A: Free the hands of those superintendents. Obviously they need to talk with their board first and not get into an issue that is not important to their board. They can't go off in a different direction than their board. But if they could free them to advocate on issues, it would work for everybody in education.

Q: Many times people tell me, "I'm too busy. I don't have time to go down to Lansing." How important is it that they come to the capital?

A: Write a letter or an e-mail. I wouldn't say they are equally powerful, but it's almost as powerful to hear via e-mail or a letter. They will almost always answer. The big difference is that you may get an answer from a staffer, but if you are talking to them face-to-face, you are right up front with them. You can have some discourse. If it's an issue that you are either for it or against it, that's one thing. But if you need to have some discussion, face-to-face is better.

Q: Legislators go home every week. What can administrators do to build relationships?

A: We have a system of pairing one administrator with one legislator. We've been encouraging them to bring the senators and representatives in for photo ops and bring them into board meetings. We ask them to try to get face time. Legislators like face time. Things like bringing them in to read. This week the legislators are out in the schools reading to the children because it's reading month. Get them to visit a classroom, give a civics lesson. We've suggested a lot of activities to our superintendents.

Q: Getting politicians into the schools is a good idea. Can you think of any instances in which it had a positive effect?

A: We have a couple of legislators—I wouldn't say they are anti–public school—but they're very pro–private school. Some of them have never been in a public school because they were educated in private school. Now they are warming to the public schools because they've seen what the public schools are up against. We've found there is a much better relationship with them. When we've got a tough issue coming up, they may not vote with us every time, but they at least listen to their superintendent. Getting them into the schools has been very helpful.

Q: Sometimes people are thinking, well, that politician is a conservative Republican or a liberal Democrat and I'm on the opposite side. Is it possible to talk with someone like that, even though you might be on the other side in most issues?

A: I taught special ed. We are all more alike than we are different. That's true of legislators as well. You can always find some common ground even if it's just fishing or hunting or some other activity you have in common. That can open the door to find common political ground. Maybe it will be a very limited issue you can agree on, but finding that common ground is very important.

Q: Do they ever ask people point-blank, what party are you in? Does that come up?

A: Not that I ever heard of. If you have a very active superintendent, he or she may know. But I've never had a superintendent say to me, "Gee, they asked me whether I'm a Democrat or a Republican." If the principal is a constituent, Democrat or Republican doesn't matter.

Q: Do they ever see the superintendent as a possible competitor, someone who might run against them?

A: Probably at some point. We have term limits, so that negates somewhat. If you're in the house, you have six years and you're out and eight in the senate. So if you have somebody who's a competitor, they would almost have to get you in your first two years, and that doesn't happen very often. I think there is less of that now that we have term limits.

Q: Term limits change the whole equation. You have lots of turnover and lots of people coming in green, not understanding the system, not knowing you and your association. How has that changed how you operate as an organization?

A: It goes right back to the grass roots. It used to be that legislators would develop very strong relationships with the lobbyists. Grass roots was important, but legislators had certain lobbyists they relied on. Now with all the turnover, people don't develop those relationships with lobbyists, so it's more important to have those grassroots relationships so constituents can say, "This is the way it is in our district and you need to listen to me."

Q: In fact, have you seen that many new people running for office run against the special interest groups, against the lobbyists because they don't understand the role they play.

A: Yes. Exactly.

Q: So one way to overcome that is for people back in the district to become the conduit for the message of the association.

A: Yes.

Q: What is the role of the lobbyist?

A: We can coach our people back home. We can work with legislators to pave the way for people to come it. But it basically comes down to the individuals back home advocating for issues. We help the people back home understand where they need to be to talk with their legislator.

Q: People in education don't spend PAC money and make contributions like the corporations and some other interest groups. Does that affect your ability to win? What is the role of money?

A: Money doesn't play as big a part generally and especially in education as people may think. We have a small PAC. We are able to support candidates in the general election and the primary to a small degree. We do go to fundraisers, usually just for the Education Committee people and leadership. The school board association in Michigan doesn't have a PAC. I don't think it undermines them that they don't and it doesn't help us that much that we do. It's most helpful to us to help try to get superintendents elected. We can give them some up-front seed money to start a campaign. That's more helpful than anything else.

Q: You do give PAC money to politicians. What do you get for the money?

A: I wouldn't say it is access, so much, as it is a heartfelt feeling from the legislator. They like to know that you are on their side, that you think enough of them to support them. I've never had a legislator slam a door in my face, though, when we didn't give to them. There are lots of them that we can't give to.

Q: Do you ever feel that people on the other side of an issue outspend you and have an advantage?

A: I don't think we've gotten hurt. We've pretty well held our own. Primarily the radical right is promoting anti–public school issues and they've got a lot of money. So far we've been able to prevail on those issues. We had a voucher campaign a couple of years ago and the education community prevailed. The other side put a lot of money in that. We've been able to hold our own because we have people rather than dollars.

Q: Every politician is "for education." Yet you have these struggles. What is going on?

A: Yes, they're all "for education." But they may be for a different kind of education. You have what the common person thinks of as education: that's my public school down the street. You have people who are advocating for choice, for charter schools, for vouchers, and so on.

Q: When we talk about communicating with politicians, we can talk about e-mail, letters, phone calls. What would you say is most effective?

A: Initially, a face-to-face contact, either in the district or here in Lansing so the legislator has a face to put with a voice. Then you could use the phone or fax or e-mail. Once they have a name and a face, that's more effective than starting with an e-mail. But it helps to send an e-mail even if you've never met your legislator.

Q: Legislators seem to like to hear stories.

A: Stories and anecdotes help them understand what is happening in their districts. We've found that to be quite powerful. A superintendent comes in to say we're having to cut this many positions because of cuts in the budget. Or on the other side, this program has been very effective and we're pleased to have it because we've cut the number of students who have difficulty reading. The success stories are important. The stories are what it's about. Often we forget to thank them and legislators need that as much as anybody else.

Q: About how many times a year would you ask your members to write a letter or make a phone call?

A: We probably average six to ten a year. We try not to overdo it. We might do five or six in a six-week period if there's something really hot going on; then there may be nothing for a long time. Budget time tends to be busy or if there's something like charter schools going on. We may have a quiet year and there would be only four or five action alerts.

It doesn't take a lot of time and it's something they can do in their free time. I know superintendents don't have a lot of free time, but it doesn't take more than fifteen or twenty minutes to crank out a letter and say, here it is, here's my issue.

Q: What would you think about the idea of helping school boards write a job description for superintendents that specifically encouraged political advocacy? Would that strengthen their position and help them become more active?

A: I think there are school board members who want to run for the legislature. I'm not sure they want their superintendents to be advocates. Or they want the light to shine on them. They would rather be in the spotlight than the superintendent. But for those districts where they've gotten over that, it would be great. It would make sure they get an advocate when they hire someone.

Q: When a superintendent walks into the office of a senator or representative, how are they different from all the other people that walk in the door?

A: The number one thing is, you have hundreds of employees you can talk to. Whether you talk to them or not, the legislator doesn't know that. What you say to the legislator and what they say to you can go back to all those employees and their families. It's like a tree and the superintendent is at the top of that tree. Superintendents need to understand what a powerful voice they are in the community. They are uniquely situated to get out a message.

Q: You often hear about the "education lobby." The school board members, principals, teachers—they are very passionate but to legislators, are they are just another special interest group?

A: The biggest difference is that legislators tend to think of educators as representing the kids. Children don't have lobbyists. Teachers and administrators are the closest thing to a political voice for children. That's why legislators listen to them.

Q: What about parents? Mobilizing them seems to be difficult.

A: Yes. It does.

Q: Why is that?

A: A lot of them don't feel empowered to be mobilized. They are tied up with their everyday work. I'm not sure many parents pay enough attention to know what the issues are. Look at parent–teacher associations today. They aren't nearly as powerful as they used to be. Schools have gotten rid of them. They're not as common as they used to be. Maybe parents are feeling a little bit disenfranchised.

Q: What advice or suggestions do you have for your members?

A: I need them to open the lines of communication to their senators and representatives. Make sure they keep a close relationship with them, close enough—and we've had this happen—so that when there is an important bill on the floor, the legislator feels compelled to call their superintendent and say, "This is what's happening. How do you feel about it?" That means you've done your job.

LETTER FROM A LOBBYIST

This is a letter from Margaret Buckton, government relations director of the Iowa Association of School Boards, after training and consulting with her and her members. It demonstrates well how lobbyists need and appreciate the work of their grassroots advocates.

Dear Joel,

Thank you so much for your advocacy sessions at our Iowa Association of School Boards annual convention . . . the session on building the relationship with legislators was so valuable.

I have seen evidence in the first three months of our legislative session here in Iowa that our members who attended that session have a different approach and long-term focus on getting to know their legislators well.

One of the greatest benefits to me was your confirmation of what I have been telling our members—the lobbyists can bring technical information and amplify the message from home, but the message must come from home before I have any power.

I have spent several years asking people to let me know when they talk to their representatives and senators and the essence of those conversations. Having you stress the connection between my role and my members' activities has really helped. The definition of my role as coach was something they could easily understand. I'm getting more information back from those local conversations than in any previous year.

Your book has also been valuable—we are right in the middle of our second class of school board leadership academy students, a small but mighty group of twenty people each year. They are reading the book and find it easy to read and understand. It provides real strategies for a small group of citizens to make change at the state public policy level. One piece of evidence that demonstrates a change for me is an e-mail that one of our leadership academy graduates from last year sent to a senator, floor manager of a key piece of school infrastructure funding legislation. Before the convention sessions, she felt that her senator never listened and always disagreed with her perspective. Not surprisingly, the tone of her conversations was often negative, even threatening. This latest message started out with thanks for all his support of legislation helping public education and continues in a very different tone asking for a small change to his bill. It ends with "see you Saturday" at a local forum, so I know that her relationship with her senator has changed in a very positive way. Incidentally, the subcommittee on that bill met yesterday and he incorporated her requested change into the bill.

Another key benefit to both me and my members included the importance of advocacy through the media. Our website now contains links to media all over the state so our members can write letters to their editors and contact editorial boards for those important conversations on issues important to education. Although we have templates to start their communications and conversations, we now stress the importance of making the communication your own and not simply sending the form letter on to your legislator.

Your knowledge about the importance of media and suggestions for our members to send articles and letters from the print media to their legislators during session have proven a good tool for both building that relationship and stressing that the press agrees that our issues are important. It also gives our members a sense of accomplishment when they see their letter in print and have something tangible to demonstrate their advocacy.

Lastly, the work session with our key people really helped me think politically and geographically, about which of our members can be key contacts for important legislators. A bill changing school board elections with potentially huge negative impacts made it out of committee and to the floor of the house. The individual key contact from our strategy session who is a constituent of the house majority leader took only two communications before he got back in writing from the majority leader that he agreed the bill was a bad idea and would not let it come up for debate.

Another member of our board of directors who attended that session found a bill that the senate ways and means chair had authored, completely unrelated to education, but something he could offer to support locally. That senator has now answered two other e-mails particular to education legislation from the board member constituent that previously he religiously neglected to answer. The assignment of personal responsibility for those key individuals to work closely with an important decision maker has really strengthened our ability to participate in and alter the outcome of legislative action.

Thanks again for all of your help in talking over our government relations strategies, helping me understand the importance of rewarding and acknowledging our members' advocacy, and understanding what I can do to help our members build effective and meaningful relationships with their representatives and senators. I look so forward to impacting the legislative process in Iowa for an even better education future!

Sincerely,
Margaret Buckton

2

Ordinary People: The Volunteers Who Make Things Happen

THE PEOPLE

These are what I call ordinary people; they are not paid to participate in politics. They do it because they love it. Some are political junkies, people who love the process. All get into politics because they believe in some issue or cause.

BILL GRAHAM

Bill Graham serves on the school board for Palm Beach County, Florida, and has served as president of the Florida Association of School Boards.

Q: When you ran for school board and were elected, did you see that part of your job would be relating to senators and representatives?

A: Not initially. A neighbor around the corner whom I knew from the realtors asked me to run for his seat. He was getting off the board.

Q: Were you a realtor?

A: I was at the time. Now I say my real job is teaching at the community college because these elected school board jobs are supposed to be part-time in Florida.

Q: I've done a lot of work for realtors around the country. They really understand the value of education because nothing drives up real estate values like a good school system.

A: They do, but sometimes they tend to be a little conservative and antitax. I have to work on my friends in real estate and tell them we have to pay for quality education.

45

Q: How did you get started in legislative advocacy?

A: Soon after I got elected, our superintendent held a coffee for the Palm Beach County delegation to the legislature. There were about a dozen of them there and we were to help them understand our issues and be mindful of them in the upcoming session. I did know that a chunk of our money came from them and part was from local property taxes. But I wasn't familiar with all the formulas and process for how it worked.

Q: When it was presented to you, what was your impression of the importance of school board members relating to senators and representatives?

A: I realized a couple of things. First, we have to be messengers. They get inundated with messages. In a typical session probably thousands of bills are filed. We had to be advocates for public schools because children don't pay taxes and don't vote. The other thing I realized was a great tool is that if you are my senator or my representative then your constituents and my constituents are the same people.

Q: After you realized the importance of this role as messenger, what did you do next?

A: I started going to Tallahassee during the legislative session. The school board association always has a legislative day, like the realtors and every other group you and I ever heard of. Separate from that we do a Palm Beach County day and that's at the front end of the legislature. At other times I've gone up there to press for some bill. One of the most effective things to do is participate actively in our state association. Stay in touch with Karen and those folks [the lobbyists at the state association office in Tallahassee] because they're there 365 days a year. I was president of the association in '98 and '99 and after that I had the opportunity to serve on some of the statewide task forces that make recommendations to the legislature that become bills and law.

By the time I'd been on the board of the association ten or twelve years, I began to see how things really work. It takes a lot of time and a lot of patience. It's a very labor-intensive process.

Q: What surprised you about the process?

A: One of the things was—and I got over being naive about it—was that in a pie graph the biggest slice of the state budget goes to education and so few of the delegates had a detailed understanding of the funding formula and how tweaking it in little ways had profound impact on different parts of the state.

We are in that part of the state where we consider ourselves property rich, high ad valorem base, high assessed value per capita. A lot of the education funding politics is urban south Florida versus rural north Florida. You have to find ways not to let people play divide and conquer.

One of the best contributions I made to our state association was as president right behind a mayor who had been president of the Florida League of Cities and a county commissioner who had been president of the Florida Association of Counties. I asked them how their associations worked at the local level. We started getting our three associations together every year before the legislative session to adopt a short list of local government, home rule–type initiatives that we could all support. We could present a united front to the legislature to prevent them from playing divide and conquer against us.

Q: That's very powerful, that kind of coalition building. How did it come about?

A: The counties started to produce these leaders in these different associations. I went in and sat down with our lobbyists and pounded on them. Our lobbyists were really good and sometimes tried to do more than one person could do. I had to point out to them it would be a lot easier to their jobs if they got their counterparts from the other two associations together to develop a common agenda. They thought about it and eventually said okay.

Q: I've worked with a lot of associations and usually it's the lobbyists who hire me out of recognition of the power of mobilizing their members. But I have also run into some who have great difficulty admitting they can't do it all. They don't want to say to their bosses, the people like you, I need your help. Another factor in many states is the advent of term limits. [*Author's note:* Florida has a limit of eight years in the house and eight years in the senate.] How has that affected your political activities?

A: It's given us a set of challenges we haven't really figured out how to deal with yet. If you are a newly elected representative or senator and you are solely focused on becoming speaker or president, your personal goals may not be in harmony with our school goals. There's a great example. Some of the Miami-Dade delegation sold out their district on the funding formula so that some people could advance up the ladder to some chairmanships and maybe a speakership.

Q: That's very interesting because it means the focus becomes internal to the legislature and focused on moving up. The inside game is very different from the outside district-focused game.

A: That's right. Before term limits if you were my state senator you could basically stay there as long as you wanted.

Q: How have term limits affected school issues?

A: It has resulted in a focus on those internal power struggles within the house and senate and taken away time and attention that might be spent on us. I've always been against term limits. It makes the professional, paid lobbyist more powerful. They've been there a lot longer and they know how to play the game better than someone who's only got eight years.

Q: One thing I see in other states is associations looking deeper into the process, trying to figure out who is going to run next so they can educate people at the entry and preentry level.

A: You're right. The year 2000 was the first year we really got into it. We had some behind-the-scenes conversations with the other two associations [county commissioners and municipal officials]. The sole purpose was to get some of us elected to the legislature without the label but with the philosophy that you were the home rule party, not necessarily the Republican or Democrat. You would go up there and stop the unfunded mandates to local government and have some respect for decisions made at the local level instead of, as so many legislators do, give lip service to home rule and get up there and do all kinds of micromanagement.

We did get several people elected. The only fallout we see from that is, some people will move from city council or county commission and remember where they came from and who put them there and others forget.

Q: A lot of principals and school board members worry that they don't have the time to become active advocates. Tell me about the support you got from your association that made it easier for you.

A: It only works to the degree you are willing to invest the time in building relationships. On my seven-member board about half are active in Tallahassee and about half are not. That's typical in our state and probably around the country.

Our lobbyists know everybody in the legislature on a first-name basis. They go with you to introduce you, which is very helpful. They provide constant information. Now on the website it's much more real time. We also have a group here in south Florida we call the South Florida Consortium.

Q: People worry that they will say something wrong, make a mistake when talking to a senator. What kind of support do people get?

A: Our own local lobbyist for Palm Beach County not only knows the legislators by name but will give you a briefing and preparation as to whether this person is a conservative or a strong advocate for agriculture or whether they truly love vocational education. Sometimes this allows us to go in and push the right button with people and get their attention right up front.

Q: How important is it to go to the capital versus working with legislators back home?

A: The people who tell me to be at the capital are the legislators themselves. Our speaker's staff has always told me that If I sent you up there as an associate superintendent, high school principal, or something like that, you can deliver the message. But they have always come back and told me that if I went and delivered the same message as one of the elected school board members, somehow it has more credibility or believability or whatever. Maybe it's some kind of unwritten camaraderie among elected officials.

Q: Principals sometimes tell me they feel if they stick their head up they may get it shot off. Therefore they will lie low, not expose themselves to criticism from the community or their bosses. How can school boards and superintendents encourage people like principals to participate in advocacy for education?

A: It's a real good idea. We offer quick down-and-dirty protection that we are supporting you. One of the greatest frustrations we had over the past decade has been that the elected superintendents—that's about two-thirds of the superintendents in Florida—are about the most gun-shy people in the world. They don't want to say something that might offend the governor or their senator, so in our minds they just tuck their tail between their legs and take whatever is dished out.

The school board members have taken the brunt of abuse from Jeb [Governor Bush] and his philosophical fellow travelers because we are more outspoken. I say it jokingly but it's true. Sometimes I can just say, "Well, I'm just one of seven members of the board and this was somebody else's idea and I was lukewarm on it." But if you are that solo superintendent you don't have people on your level you can shift the blame on.

You mentioned earlier the effect of people traveling to the capital "on their own dime." I travel mostly at the board's expense—all reported and in the public record—but sometimes I will take people with me who pay their own way for that very reason. They are coming in as an impartial third party with nothing personal to gain if that senator supports our issue and helps us get the money we are asking for. That's powerful.

Q: Is there a difference between somebody who represents your county, Palm Beach County, and some senator or representative from far away?

A: Oh yeah. Unless they have a strong belief in the issue personally and see how it benefits their own backyard, it's difficult for me to go to a senator and say I'm from Palm Beach County and here's what I want you to do for me.

Q: So the best approach is to go to the ones somehow connected to you.

A: Yeah. And sometimes the ones from my area will go to the ones who are on the right committee because they're roommates or the same party or just know each other and they become the conduit.

Q: What do you do as a board to maximize the advocacy coming out of Palm Beach County?

A: With our superintendent, it doesn't take much oil to make the wheels turn. But what we do . . . The governor started a little get-together—I think he calls it the Urban 7—the superintendents from the seven largest school districts. Art Johson, our superintendent, from what I hear, is probably the most consistently outspoken one in the group. He tells the governor the way it is, not just the way the governor wants to hear it. He tells him, "I live in a county that is predominantly Democrat, a lot of people that came here from the Northeast, liberal, Jewish, and so on, and this is what they think and this is what they want in their schools."

Q: That reminds me of an interesting point. A lot of people may be thinking I'm a liberal from Palm Beach County; the governor is a conservative Republican. He's not going to listen to me. Is that a factor?

A: It is. We all have nonpartisan school board elections, so at least you go there with the label taken away. But you're usually known by your philosophy and you tend to get grouped or labeled rightly or wrongly. So the person I need to go to in the legislature maybe I don't have the group or the label to go to them directly, so I would use another senator or representative as my partner or messenger or conduit if I know them better.

Q: What would say to principals about advocacy if you could speak to each one individually?

A: Principals are like field generals. They can do a better job than any of us of getting the points across anecdotally. They can put real faces and real students and real teachers right in front of the legislator. I tend to talk in terms of the larger impact, the bigger picture. Those stories the principals tell, legislators lock into stuff like that.

For example, if somebody took some green kids and put them in a room and showed them a video and then showed they could read better. You take that story to the legislature and soon you have a law requiring all the green kids to watch that video. That's legislation by anecdote. It rarely solves a problem. It's a microfocus and usually detracts from the real issue. The reality of the environment is those stories are very powerful. I don't like it. I can't change it.

However, I can at times find an individual teacher or principal to provide the anecdote that the legislator can lock on to and that becomes the poster child for their bill. If I went up there with some pieces of paper that said we want $42 million instead of $32 million so we can raise the test scores 3.7%, that's not real, that's not human.

Q: In other words, the thing that triggers action is the story?

A: Yes, one human being to another human being. We can't all relate to statistics. We can all relate to a story about a human being. Principals are powerful because they have the stories and they live them every day. I—and the legislators—only see it when we visit a school.

It's all about communication. Write letters. And when I say letters I mean personalized, not one of those where 999 other people signed it and faxed it. I get those all the time and I don't give them the same weight as somebody who took the time to communicate personally and go into some detail.

Q: Can you think of a time when you were face-to-face with a politician and you saw their eyes open and their mind change?

A: Probably when I was on some of those task forces. We would have one senator and one representative and one principal and one superintendent and me. We would be brainstorming and through the interaction plant a seed that would become law. It's that old thing about buy-in. If I have an idea and I need your support, if I can let you help develop it and become part owner, you're more likely to be an advocate.

Q: It seems to me legislators are often looking for something to do, something they can accomplish, some bill to pass that they can hold up to the voters and the media and say, "I did this." Do you see that?

A: Yeah. They can get reelected on it. Exactly. Senator Bob Graham used to say, "Find me a parade I can get in front of."

Q: Speaking of the your United States senator, is it different lobbying at the federal level?

A: It's a bigger arena. I feel like a smaller cog in the machinery. I feel we are trying to communicate when that member of Congress is getting bombarded exponentially. We have to rely to a much greater extent on our national association staff that can be there consistently and frequently.

Q: What about working with federal elected officials back home?

A: We do it. We get them personally involved. I work with the literacy coalition. [U.S. Representative] Mark Foley went to the same high school I went to, graduated about two or three years behind me. When we announce the book of the year we want the kids to read, we get him down for a photo op. Get him on TV advocating for literacy. We get the members of Congress involved in bigger issues that aren't so site specific.

Q: Sounds like federal officials respond to some of the same techniques, the public appearance, the photo op, and so on.

A: Yes, they do. The farther you are from home, the less you have to get involved in the minutiae. A senator or representative from Florida needs to get involved in something more specific, more of a backyard issue. We always say at the local level people will want to vote you out of office because their child didn't get picked up by the school bus or the trash didn't get picked up. If you're in the legislature or Congress, you don't deal with stuff like that.

Q: Have you found it useful to get to know staff in Washington?

A: I have met them back here at home. I tend to communicate with them more through our national association lobbyists except for an occasional phone call or e-mail.

NANCY TURNER

Nancy Turner is president of Corning (Iowa) Community School. She is one of the people praised by Margaret Buckton as being an effective advocate for the Iowa Association of School Boards. Her district is rural and serves about 600 students from Corning and neighboring communities.

"It was eight years before I went to the capital on my own.

"Before running for the school board, I had been on the library board. I was a homeroom mother doing things like making cupcakes. We built a big wooden playground. I enjoyed it, but I wanted to get into policymaking. I ran for the board in 1996.

"Things aren't always as they appear to be on the street. I had a lot to learn. It's not easy. We have three-year terms and I was just starting to feel comfortable at the end of my first term. It's very rewarding and you can make a difference.

"I didn't have much sense for the importance of the legislature and legislation. I got involved with the state [school board] association to make myself a better board member by going to the state convention.

"That's when I started to see how things work. We have kind of a rural–urban split and I found out they [the urban districts] were having the same problems we were. We need to work together.

"When you live in a small community like this, you have a lot of access. [U.S.] Senator [Charles] Grassley was in Corning twice last year and you might have an hour with him and only ten other people in the room. It's an excellent opportunity for a one-to-one conversation. The same thing is true with [U.S.] Representative [Steve] King.

"It's still very intimidating to be in their presence when they're working at the capitol. Yesterday I went to the capitol [in Iowa] and had a fine day. I called Margaret [Buckton] to find out what to say.

"You feel like you're interrupting them when they're doing important work. You have to know what that procedure is. [During the legislative session] we have to write down their name and seat number and send in a message. I wanted answers. I got to talk with one of them. I asked questions and got answers.

"It has taken me a long time to get to the level that I'm ready to talk with them and not waste their time.

"This one senator and I don't see eye to eye. We are in the same party but at opposite ends of the spectrum. He's gotten a little bit better, but I have to get past the idea that he's not going to be supportive.

"We are talking about increasing the allowable growth and it might involve a tax increase. That's someplace he doesn't want to go. He's trying to increase his power base and isn't paying as much attention to his constituents. I made the cardinal mistake of firing off an angry letter telling him, "I can't believe . . ." Since then, we've gotten to a different level. He supports our position but doesn't think we can afford it. I tried to say we are in the same position. I'm an elected official and I face choices too. We are colleagues. It has helped.

"The one thing I've never been able to do is make a contribution to that senator. We get these appeals all the time and we know those that give money get listened to more. I need to give money to him or to the one running against him.

"I feel if I make a contribution to his campaign I am supporting him. I don't agree with him. I guess I can waste the money. It's not morally offensive to me. I want his help. I want him to work with me better, but it doesn't feel right.

"I've pushed myself to go to legislative coffees. It's much easier to talk to them at home on my turf. You can get rid of that feeling of awe. Part of that fear is broken down by talking to them in my district at home.

"I'm the one on our board that does most of the lobbying. I'm more politically active than most on our board. I was surprised at the amount of political activity it requires, the extent we need to lobby, the fact we had to do it.

"Politics is so messy.

"I really have a hard time with partisan issues [when] people say, 'I'm not going to vote for this because the other party supports it.'"

BARRY STARK

Barry Stark at the time of this interview was principal of Norris Middle School in Firth, Nebraska. He is an active member of the National Association of Secondary School Principals.

Q: How did you get started working with politicians for education?

A: I was president of the state secondary school principals' association and I serve on the board of the national association. It started twelve or fourteen years ago. We have an outstanding lobbyist for the Nebraska state association. I happened to get on the legislative committee. We were talking about corporal punishment in the schools. The lobbyists took me along to talk with some senators about legislation that would outlaw corporal punishment. Then we got involved in policies about guns in the schools. Four of us went to talk with the senators and what I found was, they are just like us. They have a job to do. The thing that impressed me the most was they almost have to listen because it justifies their position on the floor. That's how they justify their vote: "I've heard from X professionals in the field," if it's a doctor, a principal, a mechanic, or whoever. If they are introducing legislation, they are going to listen to the people who come talk to them. A lot of it's for reelection. I'm not naive. They will take on issues that are important to their electorate. They will say, "I've had a number of people from the principals association come by and this is their position. I put a lot of stock in what they have to say because they are on the front line." They do listen.

Every year the national association has a national leadership conference and sends a local delegation to talk with their members of Congress. The senators and representatives have been extremely receptive. Senator Hagel and Senator Nelson made it a point to be there. When they get e-mails or phone calls, those are tallied. This gives them justification for what they do.

Q: Do you worry that sometimes they have preconceptions that you have to overcome?

A: Sure, I think there is a tremendous agenda to emasculate public education. The voucher system would cripple if not kill public education and there are some extremely powerful advocates for vouchers who happen to be conservative Republicans. Part of my interest is a passion for what I do after thirty or forty years in education. Yes, some of them do have an agenda because that's what gets them elected.

Q: Before you became active, what was your expectation about politicians?

A: I thought they probably were not open to ideas and some will be honest with you and say things like "A majority of my constituents want vouchers." Very few of them don't play that game. Some of them like Senator Byrd or Senator Kennedy are so entrenched there is no way they aren't going to get reelected and they can be more honest and say what they think.

Q: Do you see much difference between state politicians and federal politicians?

A: Only in scope. We're on a much smaller scale and we have different issues. The pittance we get in federal aid compared to what we get in state aid makes education almost a nonentity at the federal level. President Bush says we put more money in education. What they don't tell you is what they've taken away . . . Head Start, early childhood after-school programs to help get these kids off the street. Those programs have been cut. At the state level, we are more specific. But operationally we talk to them the same. They represent us in Washington. They represent us in the state at a more grassroots level.

Q: People worry that they are a Democrat talking to a Republican or the other way around. Does party affiliation ever come up?

A: No.

Q: Can you think of a time when you were talking to a senator or representative when they suddenly got it?

A: With the issue of gun control, weapons in the school, when this first became a big issue I wouldn't say there was a big surprise or an aha moment, but the fact we were serious about it caught their attention. Their aides prepare them well for issues that are hot. They like to have information before you get there. If we haven't seen the senator we've seen the aide and they've prepared the senator. The aides do most of the work.

Q: How do they treat you, for example, someone you know is going to disagree with you?

A: An aide to one of our congressmen told us he was on the floor and wouldn't be able to see us. Five or six minutes into the conversation he walked out of his office and looked at us and kept on walking. It was an embarrassment to us that we were lied to. And this was also a congressman who was pro vouchers, his children were educated in parochial schools, and he didn't want to spend time with us. I would much rather they said if you are in support of this he'll not listen instead of us thinking he had an open mind.

Q: Do you think you were wasting your time?

A: In that office? Absolutely. Still do.

Q: Will you keep going back?

A: We will keep going back. We still feel our position is valid. And we would tell the aide we would appreciate if we could meet with the congressman.

Q: Did you have constituents from this member's district with you?

A: Oh yeah.

Q: What do you do to build relationships?

A: One of the things I've done, I'm active in through our national association. Steve DeWitt [the lobbyist] has set up a website where they will basically write a letter saying NASSP is supporting an issue and all we have to do is sign our name and it goes to our congressional delegation by e-mail. I always put something personal in there like "We appreciate your listening and considering all sides of the issue." I follow it up with a note or something expressing my appreciation for listening. Even if they've taken a vote against us, I say I'm disappointed but I understand. These issues are not life and death. You do the best you can and your attitude helps build relationships just like anybody else.

Q: Let's talk about your state senators and representatives because they are closer to you. What do you do to build relationships with them?

A: Basically the same things. They are little more accessible. Here in Nebraska we only have senators. Senator Byers, who is a very strong school proponent, we invite him to visit, to come into the school. We had a tornado and Senator Byers and the governor were there. Just be honest with them; don't get upset if they vote against you. The only thing that upsets me is not being dealt with truthfully.

I'm not shy anymore. If we've been told something and the opposite happens, I question them on it. I expect an answer. In a meeting I might say, "Let me make sure. Is this what you're saying?" I expect an explanation.

Q: What about money. Have they ever asked you for money?

A: No. Never. I get mailings from the national party. I've never had anything directly from Senator Hagel or Senator Nelson.

Q: How do you feel about money. Do your opponents use money?

A: Absolutely. That's what talks. There's a huge private, parochial school lobby in Washington. We've got 32,000 to 33,000 members, secondary school principals. Money is huge. Unfortunately that's how they keep their position. They have to have enough of a war chest to campaign, to get out their message to people and get reelected.

Q: So would you recommend principals should be contributing money to politicians?

A: I would never. I would do that as a citizen. If we are contributing as a national association. I don't know if we have, I have to think if we have a PAC. I'm not sure. That also has some pretty high impact on elected officials. A lot of them are not independently wealthy. They have to have a war chest.

Q: You have lobbyists at the state and national level. Why can't you just leave it to them?

A: They will bring issues to the table from the association. The bottom line is still the politicians have to have the facts when they vote. If they have a majority of people in a constituency supporting an issue they will support it. Money won't be an issue.

Q: Every politician supports education. But principals are just one voice among many. How do you think they view principals among all the pro-education groups such as teachers and boards of education?

A: We don't have 2.5 million members like NEA [National Education Association], so when you get an endorsement from a 2.5-million-member organization, that's huge. We've got 33,000 members. That means a lot to a politician. I think our voice has become louder. The role principals play in operating a building and myriad things we deal with is starting to come to light but I still don't think there is a good understanding of what we do.

Q: Could that be because not enough principals are doing what you do, which is get to know their elected officials and communicate with them?

A: I think that is one of the things. The other thing is, it's part of our role to be humble. We try to give credit to teachers; egos are not part of our makeup in most cases. Sometimes to our detriment we have not blown our horns loud enough that we have an important role keeping buildings safe and being people of integrity. Doctors have a huge lobby, money, lawyers do. I think we are looked on as middle managers and locally we are important, but that's it.

Q: What would you say to a young principal who is just getting started about their responsibility to get involved politically?

A: Do it at once. Get started. Just do it. First, the sooner you establish a relationship the more meaningful those contacts will be. It's not just a one-time thing and they never hear from you again. Our senators are now under term limits; after four years they have to sit out. So getting to know them becomes even more important.

You can't just say we're against vouchers. You have to give them a rationale that's practical, honest, and meaningful. That makes them think.

Q: Do you think in some cases principals might think getting into the political arena might not be approved by a superintendent or school board?

A: I cannot fathom that. There is so much that affects education by statutes written by these senators that principals have to get involved. Our superintendent testifies; we are brought to our senators. He's an advocate of our being active. A superintendent who would restrict his people from seeing or contacting a senator is cutting his school district's throat.

BOB WARD

Bob is a motorcyclist from Illinois. At the time of this interview he was legislative coordinator of the Fulton County chapter of ABATE, American

Bikers Aimed Toward Education. The group has chapters in many states and is concerned about the regulation of helmets, safety, and other things that affect motorcyclists. To say the least, motorcyclists are a diverse group, from Harley-driving, leather-wearing independent antiestablishment rebels, to BMW-riding pinstripe-suited corporate executives. Bob told me the following story about efforts to establish communication with U.S. Representative Lane Evans. To understand what is going on here, you need to know that Bob is from that school of motorcyclists who do not wear pinstripe suits but prefer what they call "leathers."

"Lane Evans is a liberal. I chased him for a couple of years. Once I sat in his office for three days. He was avoiding me like he owed me money.

"Finally, we started putting wanted posters with his picture on them all around the district. His opponent, Jim Anderson, picked up on it and put out a milk-carton-style poster "Have You Seen This Man?" He would go to meetings and hold it up when Evans didn't show up.

"[The] next year, we were hanging out in his [Washington] office and he wouldn't see us. We barraged his office, wanting to know why he wouldn't see us. I got a call from his scheduler in tears. She said, 'Please tell your people to leave me alone.'

"I took a dozen roses over and said, 'I didn't mean to upset you.'

"She scheduled a meeting, and he still didn't show up.

"The first of March, he was supposed to be in Lewiston, a county seat. We had twenty-eight people, all in leathers, waiting for him at a community center. He showed up. You could see his mouth open from three blocks away. He ducked into a building. We had three guys in the bathroom.

"We finally got a face-to-face meeting and he got to see we weren't as bad as he thought. He listened to us.

"Later on, we got a call from Wayne Curtin, our lobbyist, and he [Evans] was cosponsoring our bill. He's worked with us ever since.

"We've helped him in his campaign. Once at a spaghetti supper he got his plate and sat down to eat with us. He told us he wouldn't be in Congress if not for Fulton County ABATE. He said we were well informed and passionate. And he's been a great help to us since.

"I think we didn't get in at first because his staff didn't get the word to him."

MAX STOLL

Max is a straight-talking fifty-five-year-old engineer who, at the time of this interview, served as president of the Central Oklahoma Federal

Credit Union in Davenport, Oklahoma—a full-time paid position. He has achieved what every grassroots advocate needs: He is considered a valuable resource to elected officials. Politicians call him because he is an effective advocate for credit unions working through their trade association. Here's a conversation with Max about how grassroots politics works.

Q: How did you first establish a relationship with elected officials?

A: We [his credit union] were very active in civic affairs: Lions Club, chamber of commerce, whatever was going on. The best place to start is with candidates. You need to get out and get acquainted with them while they are running. Find out what the heck they stand for. Ask some pointed questions.

Q: How many years ago was it when you first got started in political action?

A: About twenty-five years ago.

Q: How should someone get started?

A: Find out who they [elected officials] are. In a small community like this, I usually know them—what they stand for. I want to make sure they are not going in with some kind of personal vendetta. A lot of times people file for office simply because they want to get rid of Joe or Pete and they don't know what the heck is taking place on the other side of the fence.

I find they will all listen to their constituents. I had an experience here back at the start of our [legislative] session when they were going through committee hearings getting started on their 940,000 bills. Our credit union league lobbyist called me one morning and told me about a couple of bills that were going into committee. She knew that my representative was on that committee and that I knew a couple of others.

It was a junk bill, a patronage junk bill. It was going to force all financial institutions to keep hard documents of all checks. With credit unions leading the nation in introducing truncation [keeping electronic copies instead of paper] and probably the Federal Reserve was going to demand it in the next few years—it was a backward bill. It was going to create a tremendous filing problem, a tremendous expense. It was a bad bill. Probably somebody got mad because it took them two days to get a copy of a check or maybe they couldn't get one. I don't know.

I called the representative. I didn't even get to talk to mine, just to his assistant and said, "Hey, that thing is junk! Stop it now before it kills us all."

Within the next two days I heard from three of them, thanking me for letting them know what that thing was. They had read the bill, but of course they don't know the financial business that well and really didn't know what it was.

You've got to let them know what's going on and what these bills will and won't do.

Q: In terms of this bill, all it took was one phone call and you got three responses back. It sounds like you had a pretty good relationship already. They knew enough to call you.

A: I make a point to hit all their fund-raisers. I make a point to make sure I know them on a first-name basis. I make a point to tell them I appreciate how they voted or I don't appreciate how they voted. Either way, you've got to watch their voting record.

We've had representatives who would go around telling everybody what they wanted to hear. Very few people go back and look at that voting record and see whether they did what they said they were going to do or . . . just blew their horn.

Q: How much time does it take?

A: Minutes. Number one, people need to find out who their representative is. Call them up and say, "Why don't you come by? I want to buy you a cup of coffee."

Q: When you do something like that, are they receptive or too busy to see you?

A: They are very receptive. They may have the world by the tail, but they want to know what the constituents want. In Oklahoma, ours are two-year representatives. They have to come right back in two years and face the voters. I've never found one that didn't want to know what was going on.

Now, I have found some of them that would tell me what I want to hear and then go vote otherwise. But I've never found any of them that didn't genuinely want to know what was going on. I don't worry about whether I get to talk to them directly. They've got fax machines, answering machines, secretaries. If something's really hot, I'll hit everyone I know on a first-name basis with a fax or something and say, "Hey, here's where I stand."

Q: So you aren't getting into an argument with them; all you're doing is saying, I want you to know what I think.

A: That's right.

Q: A lot of people have mixed feelings about giving money to a candidate. What do you think?

A: People say you're buying a candidate. That's a crock. With the system we're in, it costs that candidate money to campaign—that's the six and seven of it. It's like anything else. It's like joining the chamber of commerce and not wanting to pay your dues. It takes money to make the wheels turn. I won't get into the argument of whether they are overpaid or underpaid. That's the system we have. They have expenses. They are limited as to where they can get the money. It's a situation of you needing to put your money where your mouth is.

Q: I have heard that your representatives call you and ask what you think.

A: I show interest in what my representative is doing and I give him my phone number and say, "Give me a buzz." He brings bills by occasionally in the off season and says, "Look this over and see if it's anything good or bad or indifferent." They are responsible for about 1,200 to 1,300 bills a year. If you have ever looked at a bill, they are at least several pages long. There's no way they can go through that thing. That's another way to get involved—let them know what you're interested in and if a bill comes through on green trees and you've said you're interested in green trees, well, they are going to let you have a piece of it because they need help in those fields. That's my way of having a voice in the system.

Q: Do you have to go down to the capital?

A: I mainly do it in my home county. I haven't been to the capital this year. I like to go down there; I just don't have the time to.

Our legislators are normally in session four days a week, so they should be in their territory three days a week. I watch the paper and announcements in the community to see when they are going to be here and I make sure to see them whenever I can.

I probably average seeing my representative at least once a week at a community function. Sometimes he'll stop by the office. Now my senator, I'm kind of in the corner of his district and I don't see him that often. I'll probably send him something by fax or phone at least weekly. Because if I see in the newspaper that he stood up for something I like or don't like, I'll scribble him out a fax and say, "Mr. Haney, I don't think you stand for this. Now let me know what's going on."

Q: And does he respond?

A: You betcha. I find people new in getting involved in politics, that's their first amazement. Hand-scribbled notes are probably the fastest way to get response. If you don't want to wait for the mail, send a fax.

Q: What happens then?

A: Usually a fax back; sometimes on the same note I sent them, sometimes a formal letter. Sometimes their office will call me. Occasionally from the U.S. [House] side, from Brewster, his man will stop by and see me. It depends on how mad I seem or how much of a tender cord I might have hit or what I offered to help them research.

Q: You seem to have become important to them.

A: I don't think it's a matter of establishing importance. It's a matter of giving them feedback. They want input. I've never seen a member of Congress that didn't want input, especially their staff people. I don't think I'm that important to them, other than as a resource to find out what the heartbeat really is.

Q: What would you say to those people who are not active in politics?

A: Quit fussing about it and get involved. We've got a professional lobbyist who works for us, but she needs us as her resource. If she runs into a stumbling block and needs fifty phone calls to fifty representatives in the next hour, we need to be ready to do that. That's the grass roots. That's where it all comes from.

If you don't get involved, it's like going into a chamber of commerce and electing the president and saying, "Okay, he's got to do it this year by himself." Nothing will happen. If fifty people put their shoulder to the plow, things are going to happen. It's no different in the political scene.

Q: Do you go to them as a "credit union person"?

A: I'm involved in a lot of other things, but credit union is my primary function. We started this credit union from the ground up a little less than six years ago. I'm an engineer and I'm interested in some other fields, not only civic fields, but also business fields. My prime function right now is to make this credit union a big star in Lincoln County.

3

The Politicians: How Do They Want to Be Influenced?

All politics is personal, and so are the politicians. These interviews asked elected officials what works, how do they want to be influenced and what doesn't work.

RALPH WRIGHT

In addition to a career as a schoolteacher, Ralph Wright served ten years as speaker of the Vermont House of Representatives. At the time of this interview, he worked as a deputy regional representative for the U.S. secretary of education in New England. After his term as an elected official, he wrote a terrific book called All Politics Is Personal *(1996). He was known for a refreshing candor and in-your-face honesty. It's a great look at the political process from inside a legislature. I liked the book so much that I interviewed him about the relationship between voters and elected officials. What he says demonstrates the principles I see working all over the country.*

Q: What is the best way for ordinary people, businesspeople, to influence their own local elected representative?

A: If you were a banker in Alexandria and you wanted to influence me— here in Bennington . . . what you would do is call a banker in Bennington. You would ask that banker if he knew Alden Graves, my neighbor. And if he said yes, then you would ask if he could get Alden Graves to deliver a message for you. Now you have to assume Alden agrees with you. What I'm saying is make it as personal as you can.

I can remember the right-to-work letters we got from all over—these dittoed postcards—and even though they were smart enough to have people in my district sign them, I knew it was one of those automated things and people may not even have known what they were signing. If you can get somebody close to me to lean over the back fence and say, "By the way, Ralph . . ." that's personal and it's hard for me to say no.

Q: Why does that work?

A: Because it's personal. I don't want to have to disappoint somebody I know, like my neighbor. I don't mind disappointing somebody who's distant. Quite frankly, a banker would have been disappointed with me anyway because he's a banker and I'm a liberal Democrat . . . if I disappoint my neighbor, I have to live with him.

Q: You mentioned coming at things from a particular point of view, such as that of a liberal Democrat. What would you do in a situation where a banker comes to you with an issue that's not liberal or conservative?

A: On some issues, they would know not to come to me if they are a bank or an insurance company. If it was something that would make the bank run more efficiently without costing anybody, sure, I would listen to them.

[*Author's note:* Sometime after this interview, I ran into a lobbyist from Vermont. She told me the business community got tired of Ralph's liberalism and that's why he's no longer in office.]

Q: You raise an interesting point. Elected officials have some beliefs that I call quasi-religious beliefs. Things like being pro-life or pro-choice. I tell people that nothing is going to change the mind of a politician about an issue like that. But that means when you are trying to work on someone who is opposed to you and who won't change their mind; it seems your only choice is to try to defeat them in the next election.

A: Most politicians will put their finger to the wind on most issues—anytime they can. The problem with that is you have to constantly run the polls. Unless you have the money to do that, you never really know what your constituents are thinking. So you're always better off doing your own thinking. Now there were certain issues I was willing to die for and I wasn't going to change. But I'm not sure all politicians find it that easy. Most kinds of issues are, Look, if you want a bridge, I'll give you a bridge. Just put it over water. Don't get me indicted. But if you want me, in some way, to restrict the rights of my fellow human beings, you can go to hell. I'm not going to do it. Those were moral issues. I could list them on one hand.

[*Author's note:* There's a section in Ralph's book where he describes his battle to get a pro-choice bill passed. He tells how he got one staunch opponent, a pro-life doctor, to support his bill, which shows you should never give up on anyone.]

[State Representative] Jim Shea was a retired doctor. I had been very helpful to him, helping him campaign and in many other ways. He used my office. . . . So I went to him and asked him for his vote on the bill. He said he couldn't do it. He was a Catholic. I got mad because he was a doctor and should understand that a woman should have a choice. I just stormed away from him. He came back the next morning and said he was wrong. What he really meant was . . . "I didn't want to disappoint you, Ralph. You've been so good to me." It was very personal. Jim had lived his seventy-five years believing in pro-life, and a personal friendship changed that. He didn't want to lose me as a friend, not as the speaker. I had been kind to Jim when kindness wasn't called for.

Q: A lot of people have good ideas but they have no organization backing them. It seems to me that you won't succeed if you cannot demonstrate some political support and that means you need to have an organization behind you.

A: That helps. The bigger the crowd, the more likely a politician is going to pay attention to you. You also ask, "Is it a crowd I respect, or one I look down on?" If you sent a crowd of bankers to me, I might be impressed by their $500 suits, but I would still resist. If you sent 500 elderly schoolteachers, I would have great empathy. I would take time out of my day for them. Obviously I would be more likely to listen to representatives of a group than if you just walk in with no calling card. We only have so much time; the more reputable your organization, the more likely that you will get an ear. That's what lobbyists do. They represent people to politicians.

Q: What's your feeling when someone comes to you to discuss an issue and you know they worked for your opponent in the previous election?

A: I'd like to think I could get over the need to be vindictive, but maybe I wouldn't. To a politician, when you put your name on the ballot—that's a love affair. If you lose, they don't love you.

Q: You mean it's like you're nobody?

A: Nobody is a step up. If you're nobody, you don't know how people feel about you. When you lose an election, they have said publicly, we reject you. It's a big rejection.

This ain't some girl on the phone Friday night and she says, "I'm busy," and only she knows. This is the public saying they don't love you and it's reported in the next day's newspaper for everyone to see. By the same token, it's euphoric when 51% say, "We want you to represent us." Then you are loved.

Q: When people are coming to you from the district, what is the best form of communication?

A: There's no best way. I have received letters that motivated me to get up and do something right then.

Q: What was in a letter like that?

A: They were all personal, handwritten. If it was typed, it still had to be recognizable that the person writing this typed it; it wasn't some aide or something. It was in their own personal handwriting. They took the time, and I could read it. I would be more likely to respond to it. I would feel obligated to at least call you.

The second thing—maybe the first—is, does the person live in my district? The right-to-work people who were sending me letters from all over the country—What do I care what they think in Arizona? You can't hurt me. So if you had a letter with a return address of District 1 in Bennington, I responded. I might disagree with you, but you got a response.

My secretary knew. When she opened the mail there were two piles. One was from my district; the other pile was everybody else. I had a certain time of day to read those letters. If it came from my district, I wouldn't go home without making a phone call. But you had to live in my district. You had to have some retaliatory power.

You have to get my interest. I'm a politician. If you don't get my interest, I'm going to send you a form letter. You may or may not know it's a form letter, but it's a kiss-off. You have to grab hold of me.

Q: A professional lobbyist you can kiss off, but you have to pay attention to people in the district?

A: That's right. I can insult a lobbyist and he will smile and say, "Wow, you're really funny today," because they are lobbyists. They are hired hacks. Although I like them personally, I never held them in the same esteem as somebody who lived in my district. If you lived in my district, you had a vote. If you called me, I might actually check up to see if you're a registered voter.

Q: Why?

A: If you're not a registered voter, what the hell am I worrying about you for? I don't have to be polite. I don't have to put up with you haranguing me on the phone. I didn't have much patience with people who harangued anyway. But if you came from my district, I would more likely hang on the phone with you, while you were beating around the bush, to try and understand what it was you were calling me for.

A personal letter. A personal phone call. If you were visiting, bringing your children to see the statehouse. The most important people were the people who could retaliate, that I had to respond to because they had a vote. It matters how close they are to me. It's how personal it gets. I always thought it was a people business.

Q: If you had to give one piece of advice to grassroots advocates, what would it be?

A: I would start at the lowest common denominator, your own local representative or senator. They will listen because you live in the district. Get enough time with them so they know what you're talking about. Ask them to sit down over a cup of coffee so you can tell them about your problem. You start there.

CLAY POPE

This is an interview I did with Clay Pope, a member of the Oklahoma State House of Representatives. He had previously served on the staff of a member of Congress. Thus he brings to grassroots lobbying the view from Washington and from a state capital. This interview was videotaped at a meeting of the Oklahoma Farm Bureau. I usually bring in an elected officeholder for an interview at my seminars and this was one of the best. The points he made about how he responds and what works have been echoed across the country by federal and state elected officials.

Q: What are mistakes that people make, not professional lobbyists, but volunteer lobbyists?

A: Probably the biggest thing—and I saw this both in D.C. and Oklahoma City—is people are very emotional and the first thing they do is kick open the door, and it's like, "You're going to do this or else."

Their information is correct. I'm not questioning that. I understand the emotion and the concern behind that. But especially if it's something I'm not working with and I don't have a lot of knowledge about, I automatically turn off to those type of people. It's just human nature that you're going to be defensive and not give as much weight to what they have to say. That's the number one mistake.

Part of that is the emotion and the anger. The other piece of that is the threat: If you don't go with us we're going to get you.

Q: How well does that sit with you?

A: It doesn't sit well at all. Of course there are two ways to look at that. As a representative, my boss is everybody in my district, and the way I was raised, when the boss says jump, you ask, "How high?"

So I want to listen to them and see what's going on. But as we all know, if you've got a boss [who], instead of coming and saying, "Hey, look, this is what

we need to do . . ." they come in and say, "By dang this is the way it is . . ."
that's something that automatically turns you off.

Q: Let's talk a little bit about what you're hearing from voters and people in
the district. During the session, about how many letters would you get during a
typical week from people in the district?

A: On the state level, in the neighborhood of forty to fifty letters a week.

Q: How many of those are good letters and what constitutes a good letter?

A: What I consider to be a good letter—and going back to my experience
in D.C. as well—is something that's been written by an individual. They sit
down and take the time to either type or write out by hand what their concerns are. It's well thought out. It's well put together. They're saying what they
are concerned about and it's getting right to the point. That's a good letter. I
answer all the form letters too, but if somebody takes the time to really put
the thought into it themselves and compose it themselves, that weighs a lot
heavier on an politician's thinking, and that's generally the best kind to have.

Q: You mentioned form letters and we know that a lot of interest groups
like the Farm Bureau will send out a form letter for members to use. Sometimes people will just copy it and send it in. Sometimes they will modify it a
little bit. But you've been in Washington where the volume of that kind of
mail is heavy. What kind of attention do those letters get in Washington?

A: Say we'd get fifty or more letters that were exactly the same. Say most
of them came on postcards. We would write a response to it and of course
[the congressman] would sign off on it and maybe make some changes in the
response. Once it was done, we would take it and do a mass mailing on it.
Then whenever those cards would come in, I would give them to a woman
who did our data processing and she just automatically typed it in and it would
put their name in.

There was a place on the bottom where [the congressman] would sign them
and we'd mail them out. But basically one of those letters, one card, was really
what we saw, because the rest of them were all the same.

You craft one letter to cover all of those because [in Washington] you get
six or seven hundred letters a week. Three times a day we'd get a stack of
mail that big [shows about ten inches with hands]. I handled agriculture, trade,
natural resources, and veterans affairs, and probably every day I would get
120, 130 pieces of mail—you just print them out automatically—the
responses to the letters. They weigh in because you keep a count of how many
people were writing and how many people were sending in those messages.
But it didn't carry the weight of somebody just sitting down and actually writing out their thoughts.

That was a lot more important because you felt somebody really took the time to say, "This is what I feel. Yeah, I heard this at the Farm Bureau meeting and this is what I'm thinking about it. Here's my spin on it." That really weighs a lot heavier with an elected official's way of thinking as far as issues are concerned.

Q: People use all kinds of devices to reach Congress and state legislators. What kind of weight does a petition have?

A: About the same as a robo [automatic mailer]. It's basically the same thing. You just consider they've got one letter and they've all signed it, so you have one response to everyone who signed that petition. When you have a petition that's got somewhere in the neighborhood of six or seven hundred signatures on it, that's the most expedient way to do it. You've responded and you've taken into consideration what they had to say. But if you had seven hundred letters that said the same thing each one a little differently, that's a lot more of an attention getter.

Q: So an individual letter that asks a question or shows some thought is going to be the most powerful communication.

A: Absolutely.

Q: What about phone calls? People call you and say, "Vote yes." They are telling all their friends to call you and say, "Vote yes." The Farm Bureau is telling everyone to call you and say, "Vote yes on House bill number 121." We've got to pressure this representative into going our way. He needs to hear from you. How does something like that play?

A: It weighs in heavier than the mass mailings do because someone's taking their time and putting their dime on it. If they're making a long-distance phone call to Washington, D.C., or they're calling Oklahoma City, they are putting their time and money into making that phone call and you think, boy, that's somebody who feels pretty strongly about this. In my mind that's right up there underneath a personal letter.

That way also you get a chance to call them back and talk to them one-on-one. You also get a chance to kind of feel them out and see what's their thinking on it and the position they are coming from.

A lot of times you are looking for a solution. Sometimes, if there's a real thorny issue out there you are trying to come to some point of compromise on or trying to find some solution that addresses the matter in the best way possible. Boy, I'll tell you what, we don't have the monopoly on good ideas inside the legislature and in Washington, D.C.

I mean, I'm a representative. My job is to represent, and the only way I can represent people is to know what they think. I'm their delegate in the state legislature. There have been a lot of good ideas that have come from the district that have turned into amendments where there's been something we missed that somebody back home caught and said, "Hey, look. Did you see this? I know you guys made seventy votes yesterday. This is something I think you guys ought to take a look at when it comes back to conference committee." That really helps, and if you have a chance to talk with somebody on the telephone, I'd say that way is second behind the letters.

Q: Has it surprised you how many people communicate or don't communicate to you?

A: For every letter and telephone call I get—and this goes into the mass mailings too—I figure there are eight people at home who felt the same way and didn't call or didn't write.

Unfortunately what that does sometimes—and I saw this in D.C. especially—it sets up a situation where a minority that is very well organized can drive public policy. There's an old saying about how all you have to do for evil to win is for good people to do nothing. There's a lot of truth to that because if there is an issue that a very small group of people feel very strongly about and can get their letters in, then they will get the attention.

For an elected official—and especially in D.C.—this gets to be a problem because they don't have the luxury of being at home the way I do. If you get into that situation, you have to go with what that minority says, or if you feel that strongly about it you may have a gut feeling and that will weigh against it. If you don't get that other side responding back, if you are operating in a vacuum, you go with the ones who write.

Q: Who are the people you tend to listen to?

A: On the state level I have the luxury of being able to go home on the weekends, especially right now when we're not in session. I go out in my district and go on the main streets and go to the coffee shops and get a feel for what the general public is thinking. Even then, you're going to get a little bit of a skewed view because you're not going to get to talk to everyone.

A lot of times, in the middle of the legislative session—take an agricultural issue—the three main agriculture organizations that we fall back on are the Farm Bureau, the Farmers Union, and the Cattlemen's Association. Those three, really and truly, are the most powerful agricultural groups in Oklahoma. Sometimes there is an issue that there's some question about and you're getting an amendment at 10:30 at night and trying to get all these bills out of the house of representatives and move them over to the senate, if there's something coming up and you don't have a chance to get in depth on it, you go with the organizations.

Another example of something I don't know much about is the banking code. I used to serve as a member of the Banking and Finance Committee. My experience with banks has always been on the other side, getting loans, not sitting on the side that figures out how the money is going to be divided up. I had some bankers in my home district. Of course I talked to the Oklahoma Bankers Association and the Community Bankers Association.

They were very vocal in their feelings on it and this one issue that I have in mind was an issue they were divided on. I had some bankers back home I knew from personal business. I knew those individuals well enough that I thought they would give me the true skinny on what they felt. I called those individuals and got their say. That's kind of a mixture of the ones I listen to the most.

Q: You made an interesting point that when an association comes to you and they are divided, you have to go out and seek the real skinny for yourself. What is the result when you are getting a mixed message from an association or special interest group?

A: I try to find out what the people back home, who are in that industry or who are faced with that situation, are thinking because I represent them. Again, it gets kind of hard when it's 10:30 at night and you can't chase that individual down and all you have is their bank number. You don't have access to a telephone book and you're sitting out there on the house floor and that amendment just hit and you've got the next ten minutes to figure out what you're going to do. That's a problem.

A lot of times it gets to be a gut check and we end up doing things that can cause some problems. We check off with other members. There's a couple of members of the house of representatives who have some banking experience. I went and talked to them and said, "What do you feel about this? What does your family think about this? What's your idea on it?" I try to balance it off that. Basically you are studying the situation and trying to get as much information as you can in a short amount of time and that gets touchy sometimes.

Q: Is there a difference between hearing from someone in your district versus people around the state?

A: There's definitely a difference because my bosses are the people who elected me in District 59. I've got six counties in northwest Oklahoma. They're my bosses. If somebody calls me from another town, I listen to them. They've got concerns. But the bottom line is, my bosses are in those six counties. That's who I work for. I appreciate anyone's input and a lot of times they've thought of something I haven't thought about. But the people in District 59 are the ones that drive the train.

Q: With all the communications you get, you must have a pretty big staff.

A: Yeah, right. When I first got elected as a freshman representative, I shared a secretary with another representative. Now I have a full-time secretary, or I have a full-time secretary for the four months that the house is session. The way the house is set up, there are 101 of us, so we try to be as frugal as we can with the money.

I have a secretary who's on part-time for four months out of the year, four days a week for four months while we're in session. When we're out of session, I'm assigned what's called an interim secretary. My secretary right now has ten representatives she's working for, so I've got a tenth of a secretary. I write a lot of my own letters.

Q: People are sometimes concerned that politicians are getting rich. How much does a state representative make?

A: In Oklahoma right now we make $32,000 a year, which I'm not complaining about because when I ran for office I knew what the salary was. We've had a per diem pay raise and we've had a mileage increase since I've been in the legislature, and I voted against both of them because I knew—my mom's laughing over here [she was in the audience]—but the truth is, Mom, I knew what the pay was when I signed on. I don't think it's right for me to go in there and take a job and then raise my own pay to start doing it, especially when our taxes are higher.

Q: Let's take some questions from the audience now.

Q [Audience member]: I haven't lobbied much but when you go up and talk to these representatives they all shake their head and agree with you. I would walk off and wonder, Did I do any good? Did I help influence him one way or the other? I have no idea. I would like to know that I made a difference whether he agreed with me or whether he didn't agree with me. How can I really communicate?

A: When I went to Oklahoma State I was in the student government and Jim Bourne [former U.S. Senator David Bourne's cousin] gave a speech. Honest Jim Bourne was running for student body president and he talked about bureaucratic mumbling, about how to be a successful bureaucrat. He said the way you can tell a good bureaucrat is whenever you walk in their office, you sit down and say, "I've got this idea." They are sitting behind their desk going, "Uh-huh, yeeesss," and nodding. Pretty soon you're going, "Uh-huh, yeeesss," and you walk out about five minutes later and wonder, What the heck did he say? Unfortunately that is something you run into.

The bottom line is, whenever you call up and talk to somebody and they do something like that, watch how they vote. Our votes are all public record.

We can take roll call votes in committees. Most of the committees are voluntarily doing this and taking those roll call votes on certain issues. Check it out.

Find out what they are doing. If they didn't do what they indicated they were going to do, call them up and ask, "Why did you vote that way?" There may be something, some valid reason, some common ground there. Just nail them down and find out, because the proof is in the pudding. Once that button is pushed, once that vote is cast, that's where the real key is. And follow through on it.

Q: Somebody asked me something related to this. It was, "At what point do you figure you've got a lost cause? How hard can you push?" And so [this audience member], she calls and she checks and finds out you didn't vote the way she thought you were going to, or thought you said you would, or the way she wanted you to. What's she supposed to do in terms of coming back to you and saying, "You're not doing what I want you to do." How can she work that to her advantage?

A: My way is, if somebody likes you, they are probably going to vote for you. If somebody hates you, they are going to vote against you and their family is going to vote against you and all their family's friends are going to vote against you. So you don't tell somebody you're going to do one thing and then turn around and do something else. That's just not good business in any line of work.

In the first place it's a sin to lie. Second of all, it's just not the way you do things. What I would do depends on the issue and how straightforward and clear they were with me. If the politician had come out and said, "Boy, I'm for you. I'm going to be for it," I would call them on the carpet and say, "Look, this is what you did."

But always keep in mind too, just because you have a difference on one thing doesn't mean you disagree on everything. I venture to say there are as many opinions as there are folks to have them on just about any issue in this room.

That's something to always keep in mind too. Just because you don't agree with somebody 100% of the time, doesn't mean you cut them completely off. It depends on the issue and how strongly you feel and how straightforward they were in their answer.

If I go to another legislator and say, "Look, I've got an amendment; this is what it's going to do," and they say, "Boy, I'm for your deal," and then they get out there on the floor and vote the other way, that really makes me mad. I don't mind someone telling me they're against me, and I don't mind somebody telling me, "I don't know," or "I'll look into it." I understand that. But if somebody tells me they are going to do one thing and then they do something else, that bothers me. That bothers me a lot.

Q [Audience member]: What would be the best approach for me to take with a legislator who has a stated position against my position?

A: The best thing is to go in and say, "Look, we understand this is where you're coming from, but we would like to have a few minutes of your time to tell you why we feel the way we do." Then just lay it out. Choose your words wisely and get your strategy in the best way possible . . . hit that kid button. Say, "Look we're trying to have something to pass on to our kids. We're wanting to make sure it's easier to pass this farm on to the next generation and keep the family in the farming business and keep this pioneer family on the land like they have been since the land run."

Hit those buttons and play it right. But go in there with the idea, "Hey, we know you disagree with us or you've said you disagree with us. Is there any way we could have a chance to tell you what we think?" Most legislators will listen to you and sometimes you'll convince them and sometimes you won't. But generally at least both of you will have an idea which side you're coming from and maybe you can find some middle ground on some issues.

Q [Audience member]: I'd like to know the best way to approach a legislator that you were very active in not supporting him. I have this problem of supporting most of the losers.

Q: Okay, you are backing the people who didn't win and now you want to go talk to the one who did win. Did they know this about you?

A [Audience member]: Oh, yes. I was very visible.

Q: He was working in the campaign for your opponent and now he's coming to you.

A: That gets a little touchy. I was involved with a legislator once—it wasn't somebody I worked for—but the AFL-CIO had worked against him and they came in to talk about health care and they came in to talk to the staff. Now it wasn't the legislator who said this; it was a staff member. But he knew he could get away with it. He knew the name of his opponent. The union guy walked in and said he would like to talk to the congressman, and the staffer just looked at him and said, "Why don't you go talk to old so-and-so; he's the one you backed. I think he might be able to answer your question."

Now, that's a good story and it's kind of funny. But the bottom line is, whenever I'm an elected official, you may work against me. I may think you're a dirty so-and-so, but you're my dirty so-and-so and I work for you. You're the boss. I'd kind of like to have your support next time around. If I do this thing for you and I work for you, then maybe you won't be for me, but you won't necessarily be against me.

I think that's the thing you always have to look at. They are your representative once the election is over. Unfortunately there are hard feelings a lot of the time and partisanship does play into this. But the way it should work—once that election is over with, it's over with.

You've got two more years to worry about. The bottom line is, you've got a job to do. You've got to represent this district and this state in the best way possible. Let's sit down and see if we can find some common ground.

That's the best way, because I've got to run for election in two more years and, going back to what I said earlier, if you like me you may go vote for me. If you're against me you're dang sure going to vote against me and that's the thing a lot of elected officials are looking at. They want to make sure that they are going to address your problems in the best way possible.

Q: There's an interesting flip side to this question. What about the people who come to you and they did work in your campaign? They did put out signs? They were supporters of yours? What kind of treatment are they going to get?

A: If somebody is a hard worker in your campaign, you feel a little bit more comfortable around them. I think you're a little bit more at ease and your guard is down. You say, "Okay, what can I do for you?"

It does make a difference because you feel a little bit more comfortable with them. Unfortunately sometimes you run into a situation where you are not on the same side with them and you just have to say, Look, I appreciate your help. I hope it's an exception rather than the rule, but this is the way I feel about it, and yes, I appreciate your support, I appreciate your help, and I hope you'll be there next year, but this is just the way I've got to go and that's the way it is."

Q: How much does it take to run a house race in Oklahoma?

A: [In] both my two elections I've spent a little over $30,000.

Q: There's a lot of negative publicity about political action committees [PACs] these days. Talk a little about political action committees and how that is different from individual contributions.

A: You have to go back to Watergate and some of the campaign reforms that came out of things that happened in the early 1970s. PACs were designed to give individuals who have just a little bit of money the chance to pool their money to give a big donation to somebody.

I personally don't have the heartburn about PACs that a lot of people do, and I'll give you an example why. My family, we are dairy farmers. We are members of the Associated Milk Producers and they in turn are members of the National Milk Producers Federation. We donate to C-TAKE, which is the political action fund that the National Milk Producers Federation has for federal candidates.

If I got that money from C-TAKE, and they came in next year and said, "Look, we'd like for you to vote on this two-tiered pricing program."

Well . . . I've got some concerns about how that's going to affect the beef industry because all those cattle are going to hit the market. If we see a real change in the milk industry, we could have a situation like the whole herd buyout. I can't vote for it. I just don't think it'll work. I don't think it's good for the district. I think there's got to be some other way we can do it.

Now C-TAKE gets mad at me. If the National Milk Producers gets mad at me about that one issue, there's a whole lot of co-ops that are members of the National Milk Producers Federation, and there's a whole lot of members who are members of those co-ops who will be mad too. How those boards of directors of those PACs are decided is democratically in most cases. They have to answer to someone else.

I would feel a lot more comfortable with getting say—and I've never been in this situation because I've never been in federal office—but say I was getting $1,000 from C-TAKE or I get $1,000 from Bill Braughm [a member of the audience]—and I'm not saying anything bad about Bill Braughm—but let's say that same issue came up and Bill Braughm gave me $1,000.

Bill Braughm says to me, "Okay, I want you to vote for that two-tier pricing program." I can't do it Bill. It's going to hurt the beef industry. It's going to hurt my district. He's not going to write me another check because he writes that check; he's the one who makes that determination on that money.

With a PAC, you've got more people having some say about it. I think PACs are getting a little bit overblown as far as people's concern about them because it gives the small man a chance to have a voice in politics instead of having just a handful of wealthy individuals driving the train. That's something we don't think about.

As far as agriculture is concerned, going back to my experience on the federal level with C-TAKE and Beef PAC and the money from National Milk and the rest of the dairy industry and money from the National Wheat Growers Association, the Farmers Union has a PAC and the National Farm Bureau has a PAC. If it wasn't for that money coming from those individuals, we're [farmers] 2% of the American population—we would lose our voice real quick because, especially in the beef industry, if you have somebody sitting on the board of [a meat-packing company] who's making $5 million a year, compared to some cattle rancher out here who's barely cutting the mustard—barely got his head above water—who's got more money to donate to campaigns?

That's what we've got to be concerned about. I'm not saying there's not abuses. I'm not saying there's not some places to be cleaned up. I just think PACs are getting a black eye they don't deserve.

CAL HOBSON

This is the most candid interview I ever had with a politician. I had interviewed Cal Hobson once, years ago, for a video for one client and was impressed. So when I was working for another one and got another chance, I jumped at it. This one took place at his home in Norman, Oklahoma, with his wife standing off camera. At the first interview, he was a state senator. At the second, he was president pro tem of the senate, the second or third most powerful officer in the state.

Q: Help me understand how things work in the legislature.

A: Sometime back I was scheduled to have a bill up on a Thursday afternoon. The legislature usually winds down on a Thursday; people go home. I had my votes. I was going to pass a bill. I'm on the agenda. The floor leader announces we're going to adjourn a little early. I go to him and tell him, "You said I could have my bill up today." And he says, "It'll be just as good a bill on Monday as it is on Thursday. You'll be first up on Monday."

Okay, you do what the floor leader says. Monday I come back. Bill is in the same form, same information. I have the same tally of votes to pass the bill. I get up and explain my bill and I lose. So I go to the back of the chamber to one of the members who had been for me on Thursday and voted against me on Monday.

"Charlie," I said, "you were for this bill on Thursday and you voted against me today. What happened?"

He said, "Oh, Cal, you just can't imagine. I was overwhelmed over the weekend with people opposed to this legislation. I had to change my vote."

So I said, "Tell me about this opposition."

"It was terrible. I got five phone calls."

He represented 30,000 people. He got five phone calls and changed his vote. Phone calls really do make a difference. If done right. If you are that legislator's constituents. If you are courteous and know what you're talking about. If you say their name properly. Know the bill number. Know what's in the bill. Phone calls can make a big difference.

I never understood until I got there how easy it is to make a difference. I know looking at it from the outside it appears to be a complicated maze, people running around, so many bills. I'm telling you, so few people follow legislative activities, except lobbyists who are paid to be there, that it's refreshing, it is a delight to have a real live human being walk in the door and say, "I'm here to talk to you about the nebulous issue of tort reform" or whatever.

Citizens don't do this. They don't get involved. They don't vote. The don't know who their legislator is. They don't know who their U.S. senator is, tragically enough. They don't know who is running for governor. Elected people prize the ones who do. They are informed and can make a difference in my life. Not just when I'm up for election, but how I behave and think when I'm at the capitol.

You are the rarity if you are an informed, involved person wanting to talk about your profession or whatever you want to talk about. You are very rare and therefore you are very special. This is twenty-four years of experience watching it. So don't blow your chance to sit at the table and make policy. The chair is there for you to sit in, but you have to arrive and sit in it.

Q: Not everyone can go to the capitol to lobby. How can they have an influence?

A: The other thing that can make a difference, if you can't go in person, is handwritten, one-page letters still matter a lot. Not form letters. Not professionally organized mass mail. A real, one-page, handwritten note about the topic.

Q: What about e-mail and faxes?

A: E-mail and faxes have become easier and easier. They are a little lower down on the pecking order of priority because they are easier.

Q: What are some mistakes people make?

A: Don't arrive mad. Often people do. They are having to do something out of their ordinary lifestyle; they are going to a place that is foreign to them. They probably had trouble finding a place to park. If it rained, they got wet. Don't arrive mad.

Arrive with a one-page document explaining what your position is. Don't exaggerate. Tell us what is in the legislation. Not what might happen if two or three years down the road such-and-such comes to pass. Legislators are thinking almost minute to minute. If you are talking "in three years," legislators are term limited [in his state, Oklahoma]. A lot of them are thinking three days, not three years.

Recognize that legislator is not pulling your leg when they say, "I'm sorry, I really have to go to my committee meeting or I have to go cast a vote. I know we've only been together a few minutes." You're thinking it took me two hours to get here and this guy's only got two minutes. That's the world of the legislative session and you have to realize that and live with it.

Q: What about the time when the legislature is not in session?

A: In my state and many others, the legislature only meets for a few months. That means for seven or eight or ten months, your legislator is more accessible to you back in your community. Take that window of opportunity to get to know that person. Don't save up your thoughts for the third day of the session next year when you have your lobby day and everyone comes to the capitol. Offer to have coffee or lunch. Speak to them in the post office. You are miles ahead. You are already at the table because you know them. It doesn't have to be intrusive. It doesn't mean drop by unannounced.

If the legislator is in their favorite coffee shop having breakfast, it's fine to ease over and say, "Hi, I live in your district and I'm a dental technician. We've got an issue coming up I'd like to talk about sometime when it's convenient; here's my card. Could you give me a call when you have time?"

What's not cool is to plop down in the booth and wax eloquently about your cause for an hour. You wouldn't want it done to you and legislators don't want it done to them.

It's amazingly not realized that politicians are human. We are the focus of so much of the evening news good and bad. We appear to be so distant. Many people when they think about politicians think exclusively about Washington. I can't tell you the number of times people have said to me, "I'm upset about the Department of Defense," or the CIA or Russia. We don't deal with those issues. We are not congressmen. We are state legislators. You need to differentiate.

It does appear to many people that we are a distant class, almost a ruling class. That leads to anger, frustration, and dropping out. Which is the biggest mistake people can make. If you are not in the arena early and often, I assure you, everybody else is. Then their issue is heard and dealt with, and yours is not.

Q: What about working in a campaign to build a relationship?

A: Most people who do it come out of it delighted they did. Then when they come to the session in February, I'm going to remember that person who was there for me back in September when it was 95 degrees when we were handing out literature. My door will be open to listen.

Q: What about giving money?

A: There's not a darn thing wrong with helping candidates who agree with you have the resources to win. In all likelihood, for every issue that you are an advocate for, there are people on the other side and they are funding candidates they agree with.

Q: To some people it feels like buying support.

A: In Oklahoma the maximum you can give is $5,000. I know that sounds like a lot of money. It is a lot of money. But any politician that would sell a vote for $5,000, (1) is crooked, (2) will get caught, (3) will go to jail . . . so why even think about doing it?

So if you are giving a check thinking, I now have bought Senator X or Representative Y with my check, erase that thought from your mind. All you're doing is saying, "I understand it takes money to run for political office. I want to help you be successful." Down the road, lobbyist organization XYZ is going to come to the capitol and may even say, "Remember, I helped you last summer. Remember me, I knocked doors for you." That legislator better remember that. That's okay.

What's not okay is to go the next step. "Because I maxed out to you with my contribution of $5,000, you are going to vote for Senate Bill 24 or I'm never going to help you or vote for you again." That conversation cannot be had. That suggests the money was given as a future bribe to buy votes. Don't go there. Don't do that.

Q: Can you think of time when a specific conversation changed your mind?

A: Back when deregulation of electricity was a big issue. California had passed deregulation and we all saw what happened with shortages and high prices. An environmental group, Sierra Club types, came to me back home in Norman. This was after I had voted for Oklahoma's version of deregulation. They said, "Look, Cal, you see the consequences of this. Here are documents to confirm what we are telling you." And so I had a fundamentally different view of the risk that issue had for our state. It was because of a very energetic advocacy of people on the other side that I respect and trust.

Q: What's it like when you say no to someone?

A: To be honest, it's very painful at the moment. Especially if it's important. There are lots of bills that aren't important. But if you vote against a lobbyist that you like—some of them you like a lot, some you like a little, and some you don't like at all—when you have to look at a friend—a lobbyist you've known for twenty years and you know it's almost as if his life is on the line, or at least his economic life is on the line, or his success with his group—and you have to tell him you just can't vote with him, it's very had.

At the end of the day, after you've cast sixty votes, maybe more, you've got to go home, not beat your wife, not abuse the children. Just recognize that from their point of view, you let some friends down that day because you couldn't vote with them. You have to get up the next day and go back into that environment and you are hoping there will be another day you can help the group you couldn't help before. Not as a payback, simply as a reality of how the democratic system works. It makes you feel better when you can do that. Hopefully the lobbyist and their group will say, "Well, ol' Cal blew it three weeks ago, but he got this one right."

Q: How do you feel about people who have supported you over the years?

A: It's human nature. I'd be a big fibber if I said everybody who comes through the door is exactly equal and they are all going to get the same response. That's just not true. We are all human. People I've known for many years, who've never deceived me, who've always given me the truth, they probably get a break. If a group has been with you through many tough battles, in my case, educators, you tend to not ask as many questions, to recognize where the battle line is and come to the conclusion, yes, I can do that. There may even be some short-term pain. Sometimes you are voting because of that personal relationship and commitment when it's a close question.

That's where the edge comes to those who know their business. It happens every day. I don't think there's a thing wrong with it. It is what drives human nature.

Q: Do you treat constituents differently than nonconsituents?

A: A lot of members throw mail away or don't return phone calls if they come from outside the district. A lot of people do that. You have to know where to target. If you have a water issue in southeast Oklahoma and you're bugging the guy in the panhandle about the water issue, you're talking apples and oranges and he's not interested. You have to know how the issue plays in that member's district. Then you have to lobby him not top down, but bottom up, where the voters are.

It's okay to be well represented by lobbyists at the capitol. It's more than okay; it's crucial. You can't succeed at the state capital without effective representation. But that only takes the ball part of the way down field. On a tough issue if the legislator is not hearing from people back home, the lobbyist is just one voice. If it's a tough vote, a tax vote or an environmental vote, you must have your message coming at that senator or representative from both directions, the professional information and data swirling around the rotunda, and he's also got to hear from back home why it's important and why we're going to tilt him to do something that's tough.

Remember in politics, the easiest vote is always no. You can always say, "I didn't know enough about the issue. Nobody had talked to me about it." You can wrap yourself in the flag of ignorance. If you vote yes, that means change. That means consequences for you as an elected official that do not arise from a no vote.

If you want something proactive, that's always harder. Status quo is easy. Getting a yes is doubly hard and if you don't have help from back home, you're fighting with one arm behind your back and you're more likely to lose.

JERRY WELLER

Congressman Jerry Weller was first elected to Congress in 1994 and is now serving in his sixth term representing the 11th District of Illinois just south of Chicago. He has served on the House Ways and Means Committee since 1996.

"Depending on the issues before Congress I get hundreds of pieces of snail mail, the old-fashioned write-a-letter, hundreds of e-mails; sometimes organizations will generate a whole influx of e-mails into our office.

"What really gets my attention is when we get a whole bunch all at once. My staff will red flag that. When you think about it, there's thousands of issues before Congress; our sleeves are being tugged all the time by various constituents and interest groups and individuals who want our attention. I always say if you don't take the time to communicate to your representative and express your side of the issue, those on the other side may have taken that time. Your member of Congress is going to base their decision on the information that is presented to them. The personal information that is presented ideally in a personal contact like a town hall meeting or a personal meeting really makes a difference.

"It's also true it's not necessarily volume. Sometimes people think if they send letters from all over the country, that will work. If I get a good volume of mail from constituents, it really gets my attention. But I represent the state of Illinois. If I get a bunch of mail from California, it really doesn't have that much impact on me.

"Obviously if a friend calls, someone who's worked in the campaign, someone you've known all your life, someone you went to school with, you see at a civic organization or in church on Sunday, there's a personal relationship. Somebody who's been involved in the other party or who may have supported your opponent, let's be honest, there would be a different kind of relationship there. But my door is always open. Republicans or Democrats. Business or labor. If they are a constituent of mine, they'll get a hearing in my office. Most members of Congress take that approach. The bottom line is, if you are a constituent, if you are well informed, you get an opportunity to talk about what this issue will mean to you and to the community and your company. Your message will be heard.

"One of the advantages a constituent has when they come to my office is they can tell me firsthand what the decision I'm being asked to make on an issue will mean to them. How it impacts your business, your building, your ability to compete, to employ people. You can share your personal experience. Your Washington lobbyist, they do a good job. But they don't know firsthand what the legislation will do to you. Your personal stories, your anecdotes can make all the difference in the world in how I cast a vote.

"On Capitol Hill there are 25,000 congressional staffers on the House side alone, not including the Senate. Most of them are in their mid-twenties, certainly under the age of thirty. They work hard; they are a tremendous source of information for the member of Congress. There are times when the member is not available. You may be in Washington when the member is back in the district or they have business in the House Chamber or a committee meeting. Rest assured, if you talk with a staffer, that information is passed on. I rely on my staff. I always joke they do all the hard work and I get credit for it.

"I look to them to keep me informed. I have thousands of issues. I use the staff as a sounding board and a resource. They collect those personal anecdotes about the impact of legislation and what it will mean to the people I represent.

"I'm asked to make many, many decisions. I remember one story about the issue of the estate tax, the death tax as it was called. I'm from a family farm; my family has farmed for five generations. I'm one of those that wants the farm not only to stay in business but to stay in the family. My district is also a rapidly growing suburban area, so farmland values are going up astronomically. Someone came to me from the area south of Joliet and their farmland was extremely valuable for development purposes. They wanted to keep it in the family as a farm. But because of the death tax, they were forced to sell one of the family farms to pay the death tax. That farmland went to be developed for houses and commercial use. Their dream of keeping it as farmland was taken away from them.

"That showed me not only the impact on the family but on those of us who want to preserve open space."

LINDA SANCHEZ

Videotaped interview with Congresswoman Linda Sánchez, who represents the 39th District in California, which includes part of Los Angeles.

Sánchez's service is historic as she joins her sister Loretta (D–Garden Grove) in the U.S. House. They are the first sisters and the first women of any relation to ever serve in Congress.

"We get all kinds of lobbyists coming in. They typically know their issues, but they can't give the perspective that an individual member of an organization can.

"I have lots of groups and individuals come in to talk. If you are going in to talk with a member of Congress about an issue, be specific about what you want them to do. Get that out in the first five minutes of the conversation. That's the best thing you can do. I have had folks come in and spend the whole meeting time talking about the history of the organization, how they came into being. Often we already know that information. We're looking for what you want to talk about. Get that out in the first five minutes so the majority of the conversation can be about what concerns you.

"We have had people come in, they start off with small talk, they give me the history, how many members they have, and they'll leave the office, and I won't even know why they came in to talk or what they were concerned about. That's not really an effective way to use the limited time you are going to have with members of Congress.

"We are very committed to serving our constituents. Regardless of party affiliation, our job is to work with all the people from our district. I meet with people of both parties or third parties or independents. It has very little bearing on the issues we talk about. I don't have preconceived ideas that this person is from that party so I'm not going to listen to them. I'll meet with anyone from the district that we can work into the schedule. Often we don't see eye to eye. But I'm respectful enough to anyone who takes the time and trouble to make an appointment to come and see me to give them a chance at least to express their point of view.

"We may have a back-and-forth dialogue. I may change my opinion; I may not. By virtue of the fact that I always respect people who come in, I always expect people that I don't agree with to respect my point of view. You can have a discussion of differing points of view as long a people agree to respect each other.

"One of the things I like to do is go back to the district and tour a facility that employs people. I recently did a site visit to a plant that made the toolboxes for the municipal trucks. They didn't have enough space to park the completed vehicles before they moved them out to the dealerships or owners. There were some adjacent pieces of land owned by Southern California Edison that had utility lines over them but space on them where the trucks could be parked. I was able to work with the company and Southern California Edison so they could rent the land to park the trucks. That is something I probably never would have known about if I hadn't gone on that tour. Site visits are very helpful to understand the problems businesses have.

"We can't meet with everyone, so often we rely on our staff. People who don't get to meet with a member shouldn't take it as a sign of disrespect. Meetings with staff are the next best thing. Usually I will get a memo if not an oral briefing about what issues came up. It's not as effective as a meeting with the member, but it's the next best thing. If you are meeting with staff out in the hallway, maybe there's something implied in that. But if you're meeting in the office, they are doing their job and they will be advising the member."

4

Staff: Often Invisible, Always Influential, and Key to Your Success

ANONYMOUS STAFFER

This staffer for a member of the U.S. House did not want to be identified for obvious reasons. I asked him what he does with the information left by all the people who come in lobbying.

"At the end of the day, we tell him [the member] who came in and what they wanted. If I don't know for sure he knows them, or it doesn't seem important, I don't mention it. He sees the list and sometimes will ask who people are, sometimes not. He trusts me to let him know if he needs to know.

"Lots of people come in to blow off steam or get a hearing. If we listen, they're happy."

U.S. SENATE STAFFER

At the time of this interview, Nicole Rutberg was the legislative assistant for Senator Charles Schumer (D-New York). Like all senators from the large states, he is crushed with people wanting to see him, and so is his staff. Only a small percentage of people get a personal conversation with U.S. senators from large states like New York, Florida, or California, so it's especially important to work with their staff.

"Many times when a group comes in, it will be me and a group of older men. I look very young and sometimes I can see in their faces that they wonder if I am the appropriate person for them to talk to. It takes a few minutes for them to adjust and realize they need to deal with me. If I bring in another person, they need to give us equal attention and not decide on their own to focus on the other person.

"People come to see me on a minute-by-minute basis. I get about twenty voice mails an hour. One day our office got 925 calls; the average is eight to nine hundred. When I'm out, I'm afraid to go back and check my messages.

"People need to remember that staff is very transient. The person you talked to before may not be working in that office or may not be handling your issue anymore. Call and ask who is handling your issue. Each staffer handles about ten issues. Several people may be handling an issue and you need to coordinate with all of them. For example, three people in our office handle transportation issues.

"Most appointments will be for thirty minutes. Plan your presentation for twenty minutes or less because what we want is question time. We have so many meetings; unless you have something new to say, don't schedule another meeting. It takes away from time that I can be doing your work.

"When things are in the media, it gets our attention. That's one way staff finds out what is going on. When issues are in the media it gets the attention of local, state, and federal leaders."

JIM BRANDELL

At the time of this interview, Jim Brandell was chief of staff for U.S. Representative Dave Camp, member of the Ways and Means Committee. This interview was videotaped before an audience of physicians I had trained the day before.

Q: What is the volume of communications—faxes, postal mail, visits, e-mails—that comes into your office?

A: It's tremendous and growing all the time. It's probably doubled in the last four years because of technology. We probably get over 3,000 constituent letters a month that need to be responded to in some way. Most come by traditional mail or e-mail. Since the anthrax scare and 9/11, regular mail is severely delayed. It can be two or three weeks, sometimes more than a month delayed. We encourage people to either fax or e-mail to our office. We get about a thousand scheduling requests every month. Someone who is asking for the congressman's time or to come to a reception. A lot of it is generic—they invite everybody in Congress—but they still have to be looked at.

[*Author's note:* I should probably write a separate section on receptions, since this is a common way to meet with members of Congress. Suffice it to say that one day in September 2005 I went to a reception with some clients. The caterer told me there were twenty-four receptions going on. This was a year before the election of 2006, which may account for the volume.]

Q: About how many physical visits can you handle in the office and about how many people can the congressman see?

A: We have to prioritize. Who is asking for the meeting? Is it someone from our district? Or is it someone who has an interest in our district? Do they have an issue that is before the congressman's committee? If you have an interest before his committee and an interest in Michigan, you're probably going to see the congressman personally, at least for fifteen minutes.

He's very constituent oriented. Most members of Congress are. If something has a direct impact on the district, that's very important. If it's more general to Michigan or it's a group he's seen several times before, or there aren't any constituents, he may have a legislative assistant meet with them. Especially if there are hearings going on and he needs to be there. On Ways and Means there are hearings going on all the time.

The congressman on a typical day in March and April, when most associations come to Washington, he might have ten to fifteen different meetings in fifteen-minute increments. We have four different legislative aides and a legislative director and they might have ten to fifteen meetings a day in a busy week. It varies, but the congressman could have ten meetings a day.

Q: You said you get 3,000 constituent letters. I assume you get lots more from others. How do you handle the stuff from nonconstituents?

A: If it's a constituent, or if it's an association or someone who works with us, like Denise [the lobbyist for the association hosting the meeting] who wrote us a letter, she's not a constituent, but she's from an association we work closely with. That gets bumped up to the legislative aide. We have a three-day turnaround on all our mail. If someone writes a general letter on an issue and is not a constituent, we'll probably refer that letter to the appropriate congressman. Just because of the sheer volume, we can't answer pieces of mail from people who are not from our district and are not from an association that we have a relationship with. We get a lot of mail from other offices that's from our constituents. It depends on where it's from; that's the main thing.

Q: Given that volume, the congressman can't see everything. What is likely to be handed to him?

A: Every week we put a report together for the congressman of our top ten issues so he sees what people are writing about. Congressman Camp, and this is not true of all members of Congress, personally signs all the letters that go out of the office. He may not read each letter individually, but he will see that Jane Doe from Saginaw is writing him and if he recognizes the name he'll look to see what the issue is. I look at all the letters before they go out. If there are certain issues that are hot, we bring a sample of letters to him. If there is someone he's known over the years, someone we've been working on an issue with, we bring that to him. We have legislative meetings with him twice a week where we go over issues and bills and we bring up letters then as well.

Q: Is it helpful when someone sends an e-mail or fax to say something like "Enjoyed talking with you at the chamber of commerce meeting last week?"

A: Absolutely. That's a signal that it's not a generic e-mail or letter. Even if it is a generic letter, the exact same letter from two different people, we still respond. We might send a standard response, a thought-out response. But if there is something personal there, "I saw you at the Kiwanis or I appreciated your comments at the Kiwanis," you're going to get a different response, absolutely. Making your letter personal definitely makes a difference.

Q: Many associations are trying to get their members to write as many letters or e-mails or faxes as possible. Do numbers count? Or is it better to get a few good letters from people with whom you have a relationship?

A: Both carry weight. Obviously communication from people we have a relationship with carries a lot of weight. But also we have a report we give to the congressman that lists what are the top ten issues. If we've heard from fifty doctors about the reimbursement rate, that's important. But it's important if we hear from the doctor's association and they requested a meeting back in the district.

Q: In the office do you have someone monitoring the media? What impact does media coverage have?

A: We have a communications director. Congressman Camp represents fourteen different counties, so we have a variety of media to watch, several radio stations and TV stations and so forth. We subscribe to all the newspapers, the ones that aren't online. We clip and scan the main stories that have federal implications. Every two days he gets a packet of clips. Our staff back in the district monitors print publications. Our communications director monitors the online ones. There are some great services that monitor issues we want to keep informed about and they send us packets as well as anything his name appears in.

Q: How should people feel if they come to the office and wind up talking to a twenty-something legislative assistant?

A: It would be easy to feel slighted. But you have to realize that twenty-five-year-old legislative assistant has been working night and day on the issues you are talking about. She's been sitting for hours in committee meetings hearing professionals testify, reading *Congressional Research* reports about the issue, writing very thoughtful letters back to individuals. She's usually very well briefed on your issue. Don't let the age fool you.

There's an age bent to the younger side because of the hours. These jobs are incredibly demanding and so the younger people tend to take these jobs. I am the oldest person on the staff. I'm thirty-six. Even though they may be young, they're working on the Hill because they're pretty good to begin with. They're bright. The resources they have are immense.

Q: What are some of the mistakes volunteer lobbyists make?

A: It's hard to characterize anything as a "mistake." Just by coming in, they've done a good thing for democracy and for their issue. It's great when people do that and I wish more people did. I think people forget how accessible government is. They have this feeling that Washington is an arm's length away and I can't get anything from my representative.

Some of the things you need to remember are there's a huge volume of information and paper rolling in to our offices and we have a very limited staff. When someone comes in as a volunteer advocate, they need to remember where we're coming from. We have ten issues just from Ways and Means Committee, let alone the whole Congress we're dealing with. They need to be concise. Are they here to advocate for a bill? What's the bill number? Why are you here? Why is it important to you? What implications does it have for the congressman in his home district?

You don't have to know everything. Just the basics. Boom. Boom. Boom. Maybe a packet to leave behind. A lot of times they come in not being very specific, not being conscious of the time constraints of the congressman or the staff, and then forgetting what the follow-up needs to be. What's the ask. Make sure you don't forget the ask. You want him to support a bill? You want him to sign a delegation letter?

That's the main thing. Be conscious of our time constraints and being conscious of the ask and coming to closure on that.

Q: What do you need from the volunteer advocate that is different from the professional lobbyist?

A: We need to have them from our district; otherwise they're not going to meet with the congressman. They need a personal anecdote or something to help us understand why it's important to them. We know the policy stuff from the professional advocate and professional staff. The importance of the volunteer is to add a different dimension, a real-life scenario of how this impacts them financially or what have you in the congressman's district.

Q: People come in and sometimes they are passionate; sometimes they are angry.

A: Absolutely. A lot of times they come to the government as their last hope. They maybe forgot to come sooner. So a lot of times you meet people who are very distraught.

Q [Audience member]: You said we should have a leave-behind packet.

A: Absolutely. That's important. You may only have fifteen minutes with a staff member or the congressman. By having a nice packet outlining what your issue is, some background reading material, your contact information. Bring several copies, one for the staff, one for the congressman, a couple for anyone else in the meeting. This is especially important if you are meeting with the office for the first time and they may not be familiar with your issue.

Q: Let me challenge you. You get ten or twenty packets a day. Does anybody read beyond the first page?

A: It depends on the issue, to be honest with you. If the issue is within the jurisdiction of our committee and it's something the congressman is interested in, yeah, we'll use that as a resource. But again, I would make it as concise as possible. We have only limited time. If you condense it as concise as possible, that's helpful.

Q [Audience member]: Who should we follow up with?

A: Before you leave make sure you get the card of the aide you talked with. Ask if it's all right to follow up with you. Is e-mail the best way? Or a phone call? They'll probably say e-mail is best way because of time constraints. Make sure you know whom to follow up with and at what time. "Could I follow up in two weeks to see if you cosponsored the bill?" "Could I follow up in a month?" "What's a good time frame given the legislative calendar?"

Q [Audience member]: What about contacting the local district office?

A: We have two offices in the district. It's fourteen counties, one of the largest congressional districts. Our district operation focuses mainly on casework, whether that's immigration, Medicare, social security, military issues. The staff there works to help people deal with government agencies to help people get help and answers. That's their main focus. There's someone there I work with closely on the congressman's district schedule. Our legislative staff and communications staff and the main scheduling staff are here in Washington. I go back to Michigan to meet with the district staff at least once a month. We have weekly meetings where the district staff is conferenced in by phone so they know what the hot issues are. They get a lot of phone calls like "Vote no on this bill coming up," so we make sure they are briefed on what's coming up. They have their specific duties with regard to casework, but we have to be on close contact just because a constituent doesn't care if they call the district office or the Washington office. They want an answer.

Q: We've been encouraging these folks to invite members of Congress for a site visit to understand their issues. How much of that sort of thing can the congressman do and how much is he interested in doing?

A: He's very interested in doing things like that. He likes to have a staff member go first to see the facility, almost like an advance visit. If you invite him our district director would probably go take a short tour. He would probably report back, this is a great facility and the congressman really needs to stop by here. Then when the schedule allows it or when he has business nearby we would definitely add that on.

Q: There's been a lot of discussion about travel lately. Is it appropriate to offer to pay for something like that?

A: If it's in the district, there's no issue; there's no need. If it's in California, we probably wouldn't go. We'd try to find a similar facility in our district. Right now it's kind of a difficult time on the Hill while they are trying to sort out the ethics issues of private groups paying for trips.

Q: Someone yesterday asked, have we given a PAC contribution to the member of Congress I'm going to visit and should I mention that?

A: That's a good question to ask before you go in, so you are aware of it. But I don't think you should mention it. Obviously we don't want there to be any impression of a quid pro quo. That's something you might want to do outside the office or let your paid professional handle that. Now, if you've met the congressman at a fund-raiser, you can bring that up. "Oh, it was great seeing you at breakfast the other day; now here's the issue we want to talk about." There's no problem with that, but I wouldn't bring up a dollar amount. Like "We gave you a thousand dollars last year and you didn't support us." That wouldn't be the way to go.

Q [Audience member]: What's the best way to get started for people who haven't tried to get their message to a member of Congress before?

A: Find out who your member of Congress is. Stop by the district office. Introduce yourself to the district director. Maybe take them out to lunch. Tell them, "My association works a lot on issues in Congress; I don't have any issues right now, but in the future I may and I just wanted to know who I should talk to." It's always best to have a relationship before there is a problem. Not that you can't come to a congressman's office cold when there is an issue. But if you are trying to develop an advocacy network, it's important to develop that relationship ahead of time. Then find out who in the office handles the issue you are concerned about. Ask for their e-mail; drop them a note.

If that person is familiar with you, they will probably give you more attention when things come up.

Q: People are often concerned that they don't know enough about an issue, that they must have the kind of detailed information a lobbyist or lawyer has. Reassure them that the volunteer advocates don't have to know that kind of thing.

A: When you come to meet with a congressman or staff, they are there to listen to you about what's important to you. They want to know what concerns you have, what's personal to you. Just know what point you want to make, that's the main thing. Don't worry about last year's legislation. If you don't know something, just say, "Let me have our association staff follow up on that."

Q [Audience member]: Do we have to contribute a lot of money?

A: Find out about local events from the campaign contact. My boss has several events going on during the year. We have a family picnic where you can go for $45 and take the whole family. Start with something like that. Introduce yourself. Most members of Congress have things like that, low-dollar events you can go to. You can often meet staff members there as well. Obviously the national association is going to contribute at a higher level, but you can find some low-dollar events where you can make a face-to-face contact with the congressman. That's a great way to start.

Q: What would you say to this group that they haven't asked about yet?

A: We deal with a huge variety of issues, so you need to excuse us if sometimes we seem aloof, like we're don't know what you're talking about when you walk in the door. We might have just got out of a meeting on textile imports from China. If we seem short or in a hurry it doesn't mean we're not interested. Don't assume we are completely up to speed. Brief us on the basics for a minute or two. The congressman would definitely appreciate that if you meet with him personally. He's just taken a school group on a tour of the Capitol and has been in a committee meeting so he needs to be brought in. Here's the issue, here's what it's about. Be concise.

Ask for what you want. You have no idea how many times people have a meeting, talk about something, and forget to ask or forget to find out where the proper follow-up channels are. It helps us to have a specific ask and set time frames for response. It's not always black and white, but it helps.

Q [Audience member]: How many people should we take to a meeting?

A: It's best not to overcrowd the meeting. We've had groups of twenty people. That's too many. The offices on Capitol Hill are pretty small. Most offices don't have a conference room. Usually the legislative staff is going to meet with you right in the lobby where you walk in. Or they're going to take you out into the hall where there's more room. It's no slight to you; we just don't have the space. If you're meeting with the congressman, you can go in his office and shut the door. Upward of five people would be the most that would be reasonable. I wouldn't bring more than five. It just gets unwieldy. Most people want to have something to say. I would try to have one general spokesman for the meeting. Obviously you start with pleasantries, introductions; then you say, "Here in Tennessee here's what this bill would do." A, B, C, and D. Make sure you have your business cards there to hand out.

Q: I'm not sure I mentioned this, but staff and members of Congress are busy during the day so they may need to call at night, so it's a good idea to provide home phone numbers, cell phone number, and plenty of contact information so they can reach you at night.

A: Absolutely. Definitely tell them when the best time to reach you is. E-mail works great because we can e-mail you at eight o'clock at night when we get finished. Obviously you want to get through the pleasantries, but then get down to business. Tell them why you're there and then "Our ask is . . ." Be bold: "Our ask is this and we'd appreciate your consideration." The legislative assistant you meet with probably doesn't have the authority to give you a response. You probably aren't going to get an answer right away. We may have to go to two other committees to find out the implications of what you want. That can take a couple of weeks for each one. That doesn't mean you can't follow up with the staff in the meantime and say "Any word yet?"

Q: Would you say calling every week or ten days would be too much?

A: Once a week would probably be too much. Depends on what your issue is and what your ask is. If you are under time constraints for a Dear Colleague letter, there's a deadline you need to follow up with. Twice a month would be sufficient in most cases if it's a short communication and not overburdensome.

SARAH DUFENDACH

Sarah Dufendach was chief of staff for Representative David Bonior at the time of this interview.

Q: What kind of communication is likely to be given directly to the congressman?

A: He sees a lot of communications from constituents. Especially if someone takes the time to handwrite a note, he sees that stuff. Also, we keep a real good tally of who calls on what issue, are they pro or con, how passionately people feel when they call, who's in the district, who's out of the district. He gets a report on that twice a week from the receptionist who takes the calls. Also from our district office in Michigan, they keep a very good count of the calls they get.

He always wants to know how are the calls running, how is the mail running, what do people in the district think about what is going on.

Q: What would cause a letter to get placed in his hand?

A: The kind of letter that would get placed in his hand, that he would take a look at, is one that is particularly representative of what people are thinking. If we get fifty letters coming in and they all say pretty much the same thing, one of those that was particularly representative of the group would get to him. Or if there is somebody who has personal experience with the effects of a piece of legislation or has personal situation that is very compelling which would require some legislation. If it's handwritten or it's a personal story, those kinds of things he loves to read.

When we were going through the NAFTA debate, there were some strawberries that got contaminated with pesticides. The mother of one of the little girls who got sick sent a letter. While we were already inclined to be on her side, her letter was so compelling she energized us to do even more about food safety and labeling. She motivated us in a very personal way.

Q: What does he want from volunteer advocates?

A: The kind of thing he looks for that's different from a lobbyist is a personal story, a personal circumstance. Something where a piece of legislation would affect somebody's life. Sometimes lobbyists can put things in terms that are very canned, very perfect. We don't look for perfect. We would rather have somebody write on a paper bag about something that is real to them than on a nice flashy glossy piece of stationery from a lobbyist downtown because that may or may not be real. But if somebody takes the time to call or include a personal story or a picture of themselves, that lets us know they really care and we will care in kind.

Q: What about meeting with these youngsters on staff. How should someone feel about that?

A: It is true that sometimes people will come here and the people they meet with are barely old enough to be their children. You have to remember, it's a real sacrifice to work in government on the Hill. The pay isn't good. The working environment is crowded. The hours are long. Most people here have a real sense of purpose. They want to do the right thing. They want to learn. They want to learn from the people that come to them. Even though they are young they are very dedicated. They are the best and brightest. It's incredible the talent we get, the interns and young people.

If you try not to figure out how young they are, you might learn something. The young person who looks like they just had purple hair yesterday is the person who is in position to take the tally notes. Very often the receptionist keeps the member's schedule and can help you get in or not get in. It can be very deceiving that people who look like they don't have any power do have a lot of power.

Many times people come to Washington and think they have to have a half hour or fifteen minutes with the member of Congress. Sometimes that's just not possible. They may think, Well, I don't want to deal with just a member of the staff. But very frequently the staff person is the expert on the issue. They will know exactly what you're talking about. They can apply your story to the legislation. Staff usually has more time to talk. Congressman Bonior relies very heavily on what staff tell him, especially in terms of how people in the district are feeling. We are the connection with the district. A lot of us came from the district. I grew up in the district.

The effective things you can do as a grassroots lobbyist are, number one, don't feel everything you say to us has to be perfect. We see perfect a lot from people in town and we don't need that. It does need to be real. A story you have lived in your daily life. If the river is polluted and you can't run your boat, that's something you can tell us. It's going to be a river we know, a marina we are familiar with.

Just come in; tell your story the way you see it. Don't be afraid. You don't have to worry about dressing right or knowing everything about a piece of legislation; you don't know the vernacular. It doesn't matter. It's refreshing when people don't know HR this or that. Our government can't work if constituents don't feel comfortable coming to their representatives. If we intimidate people so they can't talk to us, we are doing ourselves a disservice. We try hard not to do that. We try hard to take people's views very seriously.

If we don't agree with them on the broad issue, sometimes there will be little pieces of it where we do agree and can help them. We learn tremendously from the people who come to Washington.

Q: Do people need to come to Washington?

A: The importance of having a meeting one-on-one is like any other human interaction. It's easier when you can put a name and a face together. It's easier to communicate if I can see you. I can watch your expressions. I can ask questions. I can elicit responses. You get a feel for what's going on.

It's great for people to come to Washington. It's an absolutely beautiful city.

It's filled with all the lore and history of our American heritage. Also, you see that we are people just like you. We have kids. We have problems. We know what your feeling, the grocery prices. Sometimes it's reassuring when you can just talk to a human being.

PAUL REAGAN

Paul Regan is administrative assistant to U.S. Representative Jim Moran (D-Virginia). He has worked for four members of Congress.

"You want to show members that this is truly a grassroots campaign. You want to create the impression of a groundswell of public opinion. It's the quality of communication rather than the quantity that counts. [He holds up two letters.] This week we are getting a bunch of letters on an environmental issue. They're all identical. It has a far smaller impact.

"When the letters are individual and show how it impacts people and their business, it has much greater impact.

"Never threaten. Don't link anything to money [contributions]. You will lose credibility and respect.

"Use the press in a positive way. Don't buy paid media ads that mention elected officeholders by name. They just feel threatened. One of the best ways is to get local editors to write editorials. Letters to the editor have great impact.

"People on the Hill are very busy. It's important to follow up. Sometimes things get dropped or fall through the cracks."

HAROLD BRUBAKER

Harold Brubaker represents Asheboro in the North Carolina House of Representatives. When Republicans were in control, he was speaker of the house.

"As speaker I had a very large staff. I saw about one of five people who wanted to talk with me. Staff always knew to get them in if it was someone I knew.

"Know the doorkeeper. If Cindy doesn't know you, you probably won't get in. You need to be able to say we've been friends for years.

"The North Carolina Library Association put Richard Wells in charge of their legislative committee. He is head of the library in my hometown. I've known him for many years. The libraries got a $2 million increase in their budget, the first increase in ten years.

"If you are a clerk at the 7-Eleven and I buy a drink in there every day and you call, I'll get right to the phone.

"Don't write politicians outside your district. If I answer your letter, the person who represents you will come to me and ask, 'What are you doing writing to people in my district?' Someone called me from Charlotte and I said, 'The last time I checked, people in Charlotte don't vote in my district.'

"Staff is important when it comes to putting technical language in bills, but you want the elected official to instruct staff to write the bill the way you want it. You need direction from the top.

"Real estate is three words: location, location, location. Politics is three words: relationship, relationship, relationship."

ABOUT STAFF

Staff are just as important, sometimes more important than the politicians. Their recommendation is often the final decision.

Many of your political interactions will be with staff members who work for elected officials, some of whom may be quite young and have a different outlook than yours. More and more, I am advising clients to think about selecting at least one person for the contact team who is a person of color and/or female and/or in their twenties. I try to avoid using groups of white, middle-age men in pinstripe suits, since people on the Hill in Washington and in state capitals are sensitive to issues of diversity.

State legislators tend to have no staff or just a part-timer, so you can usually get to a state senator or representative directly. Committee chairs at the state level may have staff they will want you to talk with. All staff are important. They can put your call through or put you on hold. They can report your message with enthusiasm and advocacy, or negatively. Court and cultivate all staff just as you would a politician. Common titles and roles in Congress include the following:

Administrative assistant (often referred to as the AA or chief of staff). Reports directly to the elected official. May have overall responsibility for evaluating the political outcome of legislative proposals and constituent requests. Usually in charge of office operations, including the assignment of work and the supervision of key staff.

Legislative assistant (LA) or legislative director (LD). Monitors legislative schedule and makes recommendations regarding issues. Some offices, for example in the U.S. Senate, will have several LAs focused on narrow policy areas such as taxation, health care, the environment, and so on. This person may be the last one to speak to the official about an issue prior to a vote or decision. They carry a lot of weight and have a lot of power.

Press secretary, communications director. Often has multifaceted role of ensuring constructive flow of information between the elected official, the media, constituents, and public. Will be especially sensitive to any media lobbying techniques.

Appointments secretary, scheduler. Allocates official's time. May be responsible for travel arrangements, speaking engagements, and coordinating work in the district. This person's primary job may be to protect the elected official's time from people like you.

Caseworker. Helps constituents deal with bureaucracy. Prepares communications with agencies and to constituents.

Below you can see the kinds of salaries staffers make and get an idea of how various offices are staffed. You won't find all these titles and people in every office, since every office is different. The senior people, if they choose, can usually find a job in the private sector making three or four times these salaries. There is a lot of turnover and there are a lot of people in their early and mid-twenties, many in their first job. Many move on to become professional lobbyists.

Senate staffs vary, depending on the population of the state. The approximate salaries of congressional office staff are shown below. Committee staff salaries are generally higher.

Chief of staff	$117,000
Legislative director	$92,000
Deputy chief of staff	$88,000
Communications director	$65,000
Legislative counsel	$60,000
Office manager	$58,000
Personal assistant	$50,000

Legislative assistant	$45,000
Scheduler	$44,000
Project manager	$44,000
Constituent services representative	$41,000
Systems administrator	$40,000
Correspondence manager	$36,000
Assistant to the chief of staff	$32,000
Deputy communications director	$31,000
Computer operator	$29,000
Research assistant	$28,500
Legislative correspondent	$25,000
Correspondence assistant	$23,100
Staff assistant	$22,504
State office staff	
Director	$74,000
Regional manager	$40,500
Office manager	$37,500
Scheduler	$34,000
Constituent services representative	$30,000
Staff assistant	$24,456

II

HOW ORDINARY PEOPLE CAN GET WHAT THEY WANT FROM GOVERNMENT

5

The Process

WHAT IT TAKES TO GET WHAT YOU
WANT FROM GOVERNMENT

Fighting for Education

Did you ever hear of a politician running against education? Of course not. Everybody is for education. Everybody wants to improve education. Whether you are a politician, principal, newspaper editor, mayor, teacher, school board member, superintendent, parent, or ordinary citizen, you see things about our public schools you'd like to fix. But everybody has a different vision of how. Elected representatives in Congress and your state legislature want to make our education system work better and are in a position to take action. Left alone, they will apply the solutions that look right to them. Those solutions might make your life miserable.

So the challenge is to get them to apply solutions that make sense to you. That's what this book is designed to do: Help you get Congress and the legislature to do what you want them to.

Those legislators are your partners in education, partners you cannot fire. Your only option is to learn how to manage them. You do that by making political action a part of your plan for education, your plans for your organization, and your own personal job description. You may want to make it part of the job description of everyone on your school board and in the administration.

A good question to ask is, If the legislature and Congress are important to my schools, who is responsible for managing them? You will probably think immediately that you have associations, state and national, for that very purpose. What you may not have realized is that you have a personal role and a personal responsibility as well. Those associations and their professional staff cannot do the job by themselves. All the commentary from professional lobbyists who work for your associations is clear on this point. They need you. As hard as it is to believe, you—one person—can make a difference in the course of your state and federal government.

The presidential election of 2000 delivered a wake-up call to Americans about their vote. Remember Al Gore? Many people who failed to vote in Florida or as absentees were pulling their hair out. While I have always said and always will say that voting is your least likely and least effective way to influence public policy, in rare cases, a few votes can make a huge difference.

But this book is about how you can, as a practical matter, continue voting long after the election and have even more impact than your single vote. This is not some dreamy, idealistic goal from a high school civics class. I see people do it all over the country. I help people do it every day in my own business.

As a consultant, trainer, and speaker, I've studied, worked for, and learned from the most powerful special interest groups in America: the owners and workers in real estate, banks, credit unions, nursing homes, insurance companies, hospitals, doctors, lawyers, actuaries, college professors, farmers, oil marketers, theme park operators, the NRA, AARP, and unions. And yes, many of the associations representing superintendents, administrators, and school board members too. All the people who have clout, who get what they want from the government much of the time, are simply playing the game of politics by a set of rules. You can do the same thing. This book tells you how. You can have personal political power. You already have the tools you need. The fundamentals are spelled out in the Constitution, specifically, in the First Amendment.

I'm in awe that the founding parents had the foresight, more than 200 years ago, to put in place a political system that would serve us so well today. (I don't use "parents" to be politically correct. It took a lot of people to create this nation, and women were important though seldom recognized.) Even as the 2000 election showed, no matter what happened, there was a system in place to deal with it in a deliberate, orderly manner. How could they have looked ahead and understood the complexity of our society and given us a system that would allow everyone who chooses to participate a voice loud enough to compete?

It's a miracle.

I believe so much in this that on the back of my business card you will find the First Amendment—the source of your political power:

Congress shall make no law respecting an establishment of religion, or prohibiting the free exercise thereof; or abridging the freedom of speech, or of the press; or the right of the people peaceably to assemble, and to petition the government for a redress of grievances.

Four of the five freedoms listed are yours to use to get what you want: the right to say what you think, to use that powerful megaphone we call media to amplify your voice, to form an organization, and to beat on the doors of your government and be heard. The fifth, religion, may even come into play: I've been known to pray for an outcome. Who knows? It can't hurt.

In this book, I show you how to use your right to speak, to assemble, to petition, and to use our mighty system of media to shape the education system to your liking.

Tip O'Neill, Speaker of the U.S. House of Representatives, made it famous: "All politics is local." (This is also the title of his book.) Taking it a step further gave me the title "All Politics Is Personal," which is what I called my seminars for years. I wanted to use that title for this book, but it was already taken by Ralph Wright, former speaker of the Vermont House of Representatives. His book is about his political career and offers an excellent look at how legislative politics works.

The idea of politics being personal springs from the fact that all successful politicians are "people people." What they enjoy most is what Lyndon Johnson used to call "pressing the flesh," that is, getting up close and personal and dealing with real people solving real problems.

Bearing this in mind, if you want to influence Congress, here's what will work:

The Top 10 Most Powerful Influencers of Members of Congress
1. Face-to-face conversation with constituent
2. Letter, fax, or e-mail from constituent
3. Phone call from constituent
4. National daily newspaper article

  5. National daily newspaper editorial
  6. District daily newspaper article
  7. District daily newspaper editorial
  8. Orchestrated mail from constituents
  9. Op-ed opinion pieces in major daily newspapers
  10. Op-ed opinion pieces in local daily newspapers

Where did this list come from? It is the result of my own research and the research done by many corporations, public affairs firms, and associations. They, and I, surveyed members of Congress and their staff to find out how they make decisions. One survey found that it takes twenty-five letters to influence a federal elected official who is neutral and eighty letters for one who is negative.

Not every item on this list is conclusive at any given time or in every situation. But please realize there are specific techniques to influence politicians, and among the most powerful are various inputs from constituents. The same sorts of things work on state and local elected officeholders. The results of the studies vary somewhat depending on how you ask the questions, but the basics are consistent. On many issues politicians are an open vessel, waiting to be filled. Certain techniques work to influence them, techniques available to you.

Other factors, such as government publications and advice from bureaucrats, also have major influence. They are important because they are perceived to be objective, accurate sources. However, they are difficult or impossible for you to use because they are set up to produce objective, hard data and are often beyond influence. This Top 10 list will help you have personal political power. In my seminars, when I show the list to people, several things strike them immediately: (1) Constituents have a lot of power, (2) newspapers have a lot of power, (3) money isn't on the list, and (4) voting isn't on the list.

THE VOTING CONTRADICTION

Some will argue that the real source of political power, for most people, is their right to vote. Certainly after the presidential elections of 2000 and 2004, we know voting is important. I urge my clients to get their people registered. It's the entry-level act to get political clout. It's important and I hope you will vote. I emphasize this because what I say next is hard for people to understand, and I want you to know that I truly believe in voting.

Voting is the least influential weapon in your political arsenal. It makes a difference by default. Bad things may happen if you don't vote. Voting seldom makes good things happen.

Of all our possible actions, voting is least likely to enable you to affect policy or legislation. Voting is the most difficult and costly weapon to mobilize. You can only vote every two, four, or six years, and you can only vote for a few people. They may not be the ones who determine your fate. Your own member of Congress may not be in a position to help you because he or she isn't in leadership (those who control the House and Senate, the governor and president) or because they just don't have the clout.

Your vote only determines who gets elected, and only affects the district in which you live. The presidential elections of 2000 and 2004 were aberrations in the context of all the elections held.

I know, just a few votes more in Florida and Al Gore would have been president. Just a few more in Ohio and John Kerry would have been president. Governor Christine Gregoire of Washington state was elected in 2004 by 129 votes out of 2.6 million cast. After the courts threw out seven votes in Montana, the Democrats gained control of the house of representatives. Sometimes, rarely, just few votes matter. I always vote, and I hope you always do.

But in fact, outcomes of district and state elections are rarely in doubt. In the 2002 election, 38 of the 435 U.S. House races were considered competitive, that is, with margins of victory less than 10 percentage points. Only four House members lost their seats to challengers in 2002; four others were beaten by fellow incumbents in combined districts where incumbents ran against each other.

In 2004, only thirty-one seats were decided by less than 10% margins. Only twenty incumbents had seriously contested races. Eighteen won, one was defeated by a challenger, and one was defeated by another incumbent (Texas) after their districts were combined. Since 1996 more than 98% of incumbents have been reelected. This is important: 90% of people in office will stay in office as long as they want and legally can and there is nothing you can do about it. Even if you back a candidate who wins, your person may never have significant influence and may never be a player in the issues that are important to you. What's more, regardless of their power, our election process does not tell candidates what to do after they are elected.

Because of the election process we have today, where candidates usually are selected in primaries rather than by parties, it often doesn't make a lot of difference who gets elected. The people who might win are not radically different. Just look at presidential elections: Does the president ever turn government dramatically in one direction or another? No. Even though his opponents may hate him—or his wife—for what they seem to stand for or for his behavior, the fact is that we have about the same kind of government we would have had no matter who was elected. What drives public policy is less the person in office than the people pushing up from the bottom and they change much more slowly, almost imperceptibly.

Okay, if you were on welfare during the Clinton years, maybe. If you were a member of the armed services and didn't want to go to Iraq, maybe. Maybe you don't like No Child Left Behind. But the other 99% of issues before the country? Little or no difference.

What about the great Republican revolution of 1994? Did it change your life? Even the Contract for America—which mostly passed in the House of Representatives—resulted in only a few minor changes.

Do you think your life would have been dramatically different if Al Gore had been elected? You might think you would get dramatically different results from John Kerry or Ralph Nader or George W. Bush. There are areas where they differ significantly. On a few hot button issues, Kerry might be dramatically different from Bush. But on most education issues, both would go with the strongest flow and there won't be much difference in outcome. Don't forget, it takes the House, the Senate, and the regulators, as well. The major factor is how well you demonstrate that you have more political support than your opponents and how well you present your issue. The competition is less between parties and philosophies than it is among all the issues competing for attention.

Again, for emphasis, the only thing your vote might determine is who gets elected. In most races your vote won't even determine that. In the case of most issues that touch your education interest, you have little or no power to make change through elections and it doesn't matter who is elected. Here's why:

1. *In almost every election, the candidate must receive 50% plus one and the winner takes all.* Therefore, only candidates who run as "plain vanilla" can win. A smart candidate sits squarely in the middle of the road—as "middle" is defined in the election district—and takes as few stands as possible on as few issues as possible. They have to. Every time you take a stand, you are more likely to arouse the opposition than your supporters. So most issues, certainly most education issues, never come up in an election in any meaningful way.

2. *Issues raised in elections tend to be the popular, lightning rod issues, often social issues.* Crime, abortion, welfare, the economy, the death penalty, immigration, social security, health care—most of these issues are so intractable that nobody can do little more than make a marginal change, no matter what. However, they are all great campaign issues. They arouse passion in the electorate and generate votes. They are important. But what, realistically, can anyone do about them? The issues discussed in most campaigns, and the issues candidates tend to promote, have little or nothing to do with the everyday running of your schools.

Of the issues that members of Congress and state legislatures work on, 99.44% are never discussed in campaigns. These are the nitty-gritty regulatory issues that determine how tax revenues are distributed, whether you can be in business, how much tax you pay, how and where roads are built, what kind of license you need to be in business, and so on. Charter schools and vouchers come up from time to time but are seldom decisive in elections. An average legislature may consider 2,000 to 5,000 bills in an annual session. Most touch only a few people, although for them, the impact can be terrific.

For instance, you could be selling real estate and the government wants you to take responsibility for informing buyers about potential or real defects in houses. You could be a banker and some legislator decides that all financial institutions must return original checks rather than the computer images you've been using. Perhaps you are an emergency room physician and you can't get paid because of insurance company rules. Maybe somebody thinks it's a good idea to ban drink machines in schools. These issues are almost never discussed in campaigns and no election is ever decided because of them.

Think voters really care about issues? The *Washington Post* reported a conversation with two voters who had made up their minds. One told a candidate, "I knew I was going to vote for you because of the handshake." He couldn't name a single issue she favored, but he admired her confidence. "You can tell something about a person from a handshake."

Another voter said, "I was impressed that she thinks she can make a difference in education. I haven't voted in a while. But I haven't had anyone knock on my door." This voter did not ask what kind of difference the candidate would make in education.

3. In fact, issues very seldom determine elections. Most people who get elected win because of name recognition and personality. They are well known and liked. In 1998, a pro wrestler turned radio talk show host named Jesse Ventura became governor of Minnesota; he was well known and likable. He said all the right things. Could he govern? Where did he stand on issues? Most people, even those who voted for him, didn't know or care. Frequently voters project their feelings and values onto candidates they like without actually knowing what the candidate believes, just as they think they know movie stars from the characters they play.

Some candidates happen to do a particularly good job of promoting one of those insoluble social issues and ride into office. If those elected the first time have any particular knowledge of how politics really works or know anything about education issues, that is a fortuitous accident. I recall a woman I knew in Davidson, North Carolina, who got incensed about something in her children's school. She went down and signed up to run for city council. Within a week, she had withdrawn. She found out the city council had no responsibility for the school and no authority to do anything about it.

4. We don't always get the best and brightest running for office, especially at the state and local level. People who run for political office are often those with little or no experience in education or anything else. One reason is that anyone who wants or needs to make significant money cannot afford to be in politics. The job is demanding and, in most states, the pay is lousy. ("Lousy pay" depends on your perspective. One state representative in Missouri told one of my seminar audiences he ran for office because he was going broke on his farm and didn't know what else to do.)

I am constantly surprised, therefore, at the significant number of talented, bright people who run for public office out of a sense of responsibility and desire to do good. Why they would do so is a mystery, given the thanks they usually get from the people and the media.

5. *Historically, something more than 90% of incumbents will get reelected and there is nothing you or anyone else can do about it.* Unless they really mess up, they are in office as long as they want to be. Understanding and accepting the above five points is a crucial step to achieving political power for yourself. It is key to the power exercised by professional lobbyists and special interest groups. They know that it is not who gets elected that decides most issues. They know that most elections are decided on personalities and name recognition, not issues.

Professional lobbyists know that most elected officials come into office, and many remain in office, ignorant of most issues. This is not to criticize them but to recognize reality. They cannot know much about many issues because there are too many.

Smart lobbyists and special interest groups also know, therefore, that it is what they do after the election that will determine their success at getting what they want from the political system. Political professionals and smart organizations will frequently support both sides in an election in order to build a relationship with whoever wins. They understand that the point of supporting candidates is less to get someone to win, though that's great when it happens, and more to have a relationship with whoever wins.

One state representative in Florida has participated in several of my seminars training people how to lobby. He always tells the story about when he was first elected. He asked an experienced elected official what politics is all about. The old pro said, "Politics is just a matter of who gets what, when."

"I was discouraged," my friend said. "I didn't want to believe that." But now, after several terms in office, he knows it is true. I learned reality in a different way. In 1992, I ran for state house of representatives in a district in Charlotte, North Carolina. I was full of idealism and eager to make the system work better. An old pro I consulted also told me something I didn't want to believe. "Don't spend a lot of time studying the issues," he said. "Nobody will ask you about them, and that's not going to win the election anyway."

It was discouraging but true. I have talked about this with many, many people in office. They almost all agree there is a lot of truth in the statement: Issues seldom win or lose elections. When they do, these issues do not tend to be education issues but issues that probably aren't solvable in the political system.

In my own campaign, after advertising, going door to door, and being interviewed by the media, I received only eleven phone calls from my 24,000 potential voters. Ten were from an organized antiabortion lobby. One was from a concerned citizen who wanted to hear my stand on issues. One.

Most elected officials enter office as an empty vessel. They are ignorant. While they have campaigned on some issues, including being "for education," they probably don't know about your education issues and they probably don't care. They may never know or care about your issues unless you develop personal political power.

Don't be discouraged. It doesn't mean that they can't or won't help you. It doesn't mean our system of democracy is failing. In fact, if anything, this is the root of our salvation and the reason I retain a deep and abiding faith in our democracy.

Because there is one thing politicians do care about, getting elected and reelected, that is and should be their primary goal. Many people will say with disdain, "She only wants to get elected." Of course she does. Politicians' behavior is shaped by a desire to be elected. That gives you power.

You see, although they may not know or care about your issues, you can get them to care about you, especially when you live or work in their district and are therefore a constituent. You are one of theirs if you work in a school in their district or live in their district. If you work in one district and live in another, you have a twofer: two sets of politicians who can care about you.

The most powerful moment in politics is when a voter talks with the person for whom they can vote. It's true during the campaign. It's true after they win. Members of the U.S. House and many state legislatures run for office every two years. That means they are always looking over their shoulder for someone who might run against them and looking ahead for voters in the next election.

It is hard to understand this if you have not run for office. But I can tell you that someone who is campaigning will give his or her full attention to a voter. If you can vote for me, you will have my undivided attention. You can do something most professional lobbyists and no special interest group can do: You can vote for me. I not only want your vote; I lust for it and, just as important, the approval it represents. (See Ralph Wright's comments in "The Pros.") I have asked hundreds of state and federal elected officials across the country and they all confirm this effect. When running for or serving in office, you lust not only for contact but also for approval. Your eyes are always on the next election, and any voter who gets irritated could start a ripple across the district. (U.S. senators are a possible exception, since they only run every six years. But even they must keep a wary eye over their shoulder, especially in the two years before an election.)

You may be wondering how I can say this and say that casting your vote is the least important weapon in your political arsenal.

In most cases your vote really isn't going to make a difference, unless you and many others don't vote. I'm sorry, but your vote is probably very predictable just as is mine and everybody else's. You've heard of the red states and the blue states and red districts and blue districts. They are predictably Republican or Democratic. Most U.S. House districts and state house and senate districts are predictable because they have been designed to reelect the incumbent, or someone just like them. In presidential and governor elections, the election will be decided by the 5% or so of swing voters, those who vote for a Democrat sometimes, a Republican sometimes, or even an independent.

But it is the lust of elected officials for election and for approval by voters—all voters—that is your most important weapon. They don't know how you voted. They don't know how anyone is going to vote. All they know is that they have to try to convert every person they meet into a supporter.

It would be difficult to overstate the urgent drive in a politician to win support and love and admiration from every person who can cast a vote. Face it: Candidates and elected officials may never know or care about your issues. Your best option is to make them care about you and what you can do to elect them. Then they may care about your issues.

In the following pages, I'll show you how smart individuals and organizations do it, emphasizing three major areas: (1) attitude, (2) relationship, and (3) message. You'll notice one thing is missing: that chart you may have seen titled "How a Bill Moves Through the Legislature." I don't care if you don't know how that works. Don't waste your time trying to learn the process. I'll tell you how to get around that.

More important is the principle that you are going to build the right kind of long-term relationship with the people you can vote for. Then use that relationship under the direction of people in your association who really know "how a bill moves through the legislature." Let them tell you what to do and when to do it, and you will be all right.

A REFLECTION

As I was closing a seminar in Washington once, a woman stood up to get my attention, very agitated. I thought she was angry. "Joel," she shouted, "you left something out." She went on to explain that she had been in my seminar the year before and I said something that changed her life.

"You told us last year that the people who write the letters write the laws. I took it to heart and went home and started writing letters and it's true. They pay attention." The audience applauded. All I could do was thank her.

I appreciated the endorsement, and it sounds like something I would say because I believe it. But to be honest, I did not remember saying that, although I have many times since.

6

Attitude: How to Get Your Mind in the Right Place

YOUR ATTITUDE ABOUT POLITICS

In politics, as in the rest of your life, attitude can sink or save you. When I start working with a group of people who want to win in politics, one of the first things I do is play a word-association game. I ask them to give me the first word that pops into their mind when I say "politics." When a group responds with "sleaze," "crooked," "selfish," "greed," and other negative words, then I know I am speaking to people with very little political experience.

Other groups, often those who are most successful at getting what they want from the government, respond with words like "caring," "sincere," "dedicated," "hardworking," and "honest." Two things become obvious immediately: (1) People with little experience in politics have a negative image of politics, and (2) most people who participate in the system have a positive image.

Why is that? How is it that the people who are in direct contact feel good, and the ones out of touch feel bad? How can they feel so bad about something they have no direct experience with?

After hearing this enough, I started asking focus groups questions such as "Since you really haven't been involved, what causes you to form this opinion about politics?" The answer always came back loud and clear: the media. People who feel negative about politics have accepted what they read in the newspapers and see on television.

In case you have negative feelings about politics and politicians, let me offer a few thoughts. Consider the things you know about—your school board, school system, or school. Do the media do a good job of reporting on these things? Do they give a thorough, complete, and accurate report?

117

If you only read the newspapers and watched TV, would you have an accurate impression about the business of education as you know it?

Unless you're highly unusual, the answer is "Absolutely not." That's because the media report on the exceptional, the unusual, the entertaining, the failures. The media folks, and I used to be one, look for controversy, conflict, and contention.

It doesn't meet their definition of news to report that a member of Congress or the state legislature works hard, serves the district well, listens to the constituents, and tries to make rational sense out of a lot of complex problems. It is seldom news that teachers teach and children learn. It's not news that a member of your legislature is honest.

The news you get about politics is like much of the news you get about everything else—all you get is the exceptional, which often means the failures. What you have constantly hammered into your consciousness are the failures of our political system.

But there's another even more important effect that contributes to the negativity many people feel about politics. Much of what is reported about politics is about campaigns. Campaigns are by nature adversarial, controversial. The story is portrayed as drama focused on conflict and contention. This is called the horse race story: who's up, who's down, who's ahead, who scored, who didn't.

If you are campaigning, the name of the game is to slam your opponent. It's like football. It's a contact sport. It's rough and people get hurt. I don't mean to defend negative campaigning. But it is important to recognize that it is campaigning—and media coverage of it—that largely creates the negative perception about all politics. Don't forget: Campaigns have little or nothing to do with most issues that you and I care about. In fact, campaigns have very little to do with what government does.

Don't get me wrong—campaigns are important. Voting is important. But campaigns and voting only decide which men and women will serve in office. Very few issues are decided in elections.

Elections are not what we are talking about. What we are talking about—lobbying by grassroots volunteers—is what happens between the elections. What happens after you vote? Grassroots lobbying has almost nothing to do with the things you see on TV or read in the newspapers.

Grassroots lobbying is a civilized, orderly, businesslike transaction. That's why you don't read about it or see it on TV. It may seem dull, but it gets things done. Believe me, it will feel much more like the day-to-day business of education. It should—it is part of your work.

When you vote on election day, that's like the day you decide who gets hired or, really, who gets elected. The next day, your mostly unlearned, unskilled new employees, your senators or representatives, report to work. Their success is determined by what happens in the ensuing weeks and months after being hired. You need to give your newly elected officials constant direction and coaching. Just getting elected does not mean the voters, or anybody else, has told them what to do, despite comments about "the voters have spoken" or "the voters have given me a mandate." (President Bush won fair and square, but I don't think 51% of the vote is a mandate.)

Even if they do have any kind of "mandate" it will only be one issue, and that's probably not your issue. You still have to tell them what you want. If you don't, you leave them free to do whatever they choose. More significantly, they will undoubtedly be hearing from people on the other side of your issues, and if they don't hear from you, you give them permission to go the other way.

YOUR ATTITUDE ABOUT ADVOCACY

In our research into why people don't contact elected officials, one comment came up frequently: "Elected officials are too busy doing important work to talk with me." It's true they are busy. But nothing is more important to an elected official than a constituent. Just think, Who puts him or her in office? Who is going to determine if he or she stays in office? You and others like you who vote in the district.

I did a grassroots training session in New York state not long ago. Then I went with one of the trainees over to the capitol to meet with her senator. When we got there, we met with a staffer who said the senator would be back shortly; he was in a meeting.

The senator was Ronald B. Stafford, chairman of the Senate Finance Committee. He was holding an important budget hearing, yet he left the meeting to come talk with this one woman from the district. When it was over, I asked him why he left an important meeting to meet with just one voter. Here is what he said: "Because I know that anytime I don't meet with her or any of my constituents, they are going to go back home and get on the phone and call everyone they know and tell them that I'm getting too big for my britches and I have no time for someone back home. And the next election, they may send me back home." Elected officials know, and they constantly keep in mind, who sent them to the capital and who can send them home.

Many people think politicians don't want to hear what they have to say because the politicians have already made up their minds. On some issues, it's true; you can't change their minds. Elected officials, just like you and me, have some attitudes they will not change. I call these quasi-religious beliefs. They are deeply seated matters of faith and belief, and almost no amount of logic or persuasion will change a person's belief system. Abortion, gun control, the death penalty—you are unlikely to change anyone's mind on those sorts of issues. Many times, not even the threat of losing an election can change a politician's mind about these issues; they would rather lose than change.

But the education issues you will be lobbying on are more technical and less visible. They are less a matter of faith than of practicality. You are concerned about regulatory matters or some tax or budget item. This sort of issue is not likely to be discussed in a campaign and isn't likely to become part of a campaign.

Your elected official probably knows little or nothing about the issue and really doesn't care. They are waiting to be informed and persuaded. These are the 99.44% of issues that take up time in state legislatures and the Congress. Any of them could probably be decided any way and the republic would survive just fine.

This is true of most education issues. History is unlikely to change regardless of which way your senator or representative votes. Politicians are willing to listen to any sensible suggestion for a change in the regulations. They have no emotional or political stake to defend and are willing to be persuaded.

Remember, since most issues never come up in a campaign and they haven't learned about them some other way, elected officials go into office as empty vessels—they don't know your issue and they don't care. They can vote whichever way the wind is blowing or whichever way someone nudges them. Somebody is going to help them decide what they think. It can be you, particularly if you live or work in their district. You can create or change their opinion.

But first, you have to persuade them to care at all. If you can convince them that enough voters in their district or enough important people in the district care—they will care. Then you have a chance to persuade them to support your position. That's a main source of power for you. (I will explain how you can become important to your elected official when we get to relationship building.)

You can make a difference because you vote in their district or work in their district and have contacts there. They care about you and what you think, even if they don't know or care about your issue. Elected officials want you to go home and brag to everyone that you talked to them and they listened to what you had to say. Even people who belong to special interest groups often fail to realize their own power. They tend to think they don't need to work for themselves because they have a paid professional lobbyist to do the work.

As a member of a school board association or a principal's association, you probably have a professional lobbyist. You need that professional, the one I call the "inside lobbyist." But that lobbyist cannot vote except in one district. The professional has the power of knowledge, persuasion, personal relationship, good information, and maybe fund-raising—and that's significant. But the importance of the professional lobbyist pales in comparison to someone who lives and votes or works in the district.

Look at it from the standpoint of an elected official. Imagine that I am your senator. I may like your professional lobbyist. I may respect the lobbyist. But she needs me more than I need her. I can accept her information, reject it, or just ignore it. If I kiss off or ignore your lobbyist, so what? That lobbyist can hardly try to get even with me for fear that I will remember it the next time she needs me.

But as your senator, when someone who can vote for me says people in my district care about an issue, I have to listen if I want to stay in office. I can't afford to have people back home saying I don't care. If you are a school board member or a principal, I have to respect your position power. You are a substantial member of my community and not only do I want you saying positive things about me, I really, really don't want you saying negative things.

What's more, you can help me understand why something is important in my district. After all, what I want to do is represent that district. Perhaps you don't advocate for your issues because you are worried about getting into controversy and somehow someone will retaliate. You are concerned that something bad will happen as a result. It's just not likely.

Think about the issues you are discussing. How much risk is there in taking a stand on computers in the classroom? Vending machines in the schools? Teacher qualifications? Testing students? These issues are not like abortion or gun control, where everybody has an opinion and strong feelings.

Most education issues are not the kind of thing anyone will get emotional about. No one except you and your opponents care. Most issues never even make the back section of the newspaper, much less the television.

Obviously if you work for a school system, you may not be able to be as public as you would want and you need to be careful. But as long as you stick to issues and avoid personal references, it's hard to imagine any negative result. Even the most nonpartisan, apolitical group is expected to advocate or educate to win support for its goals. Politicians want and need your expertise and experience. Recognize the difference between supporting issues and candidates. As long as you stick to your issues and skip personalities and endorsing candidates, you will stay out of trouble. Despite media reports to the contrary, Americans are usually able to disagree agreeably. The media folks have to emphasize conflict and maximize the appearance of conflict or they lose their audience. Do not accept the media portrayal of politics as reality.

Another obstacle to advocacy is time. We're all so busy surviving, dealing with family and jobs that we think we don't have time to get involved in politics. You may envision "getting involved" as having to stay on the phone, go to a lot of meetings, write a lot of letters, and travel to the capital. Not so.

If you are focused on one issue, you probably won't need to write or call more than six times as the legislation moves through the process. If you make contact six times, taking less than a half hour each time, you can have significant impact. How long does it take to scribble a note and fax it or to make a phone call urging support?

As a key contact for your association, it would be a busy year indeed if you were asked to contact your elected official more than ten times. That means, unless things are really hopping, you might be asked to make ten phone calls or write ten letters. That's it. Figuring a maximum of one-half hour each, you have invested five hours.

Most key contacts write fewer than four letters and make fewer than four calls or personal contacts. Even if you double or triple it, you aren't risking overload. Aren't you willing to commit five to fifteen hours in the next twelve months to achieve your political goals for education?

If everyone who has a stake in your issue would commit those few hours, you would be unstoppable. You would have an unbeatable political machine. That's without even leaving your office. As for going to the capital, it can be useful and fun, but it's not necessary.

In fact, when you become a volunteer advocate for your association, your best work is done at home in the district. You drink coffee with your elected official, you attend meetings, you invite the politicians to come into your school, and you represent your association in the district. These contacts are much more powerful coming, as they do, from constituents in the home district. They don't take much time or travel and lots of good work is accomplished during times and in places that you are doing other things anyway.

As we researched the reasons average citizens don't get involved in lobbying, one answer came up time and time again that surprised me. "The buildings intimidate me." I chuckled the first time I heard this. But then as my focus group work proceeded, it became obvious—the buildings are a factor in alienating people. Of course, as I said, you don't have to go to the capitol or other government buildings. But there are times when it's useful. You will find it's fun.

But to get over that intimidation factor I started asking the question, "What is it about the buildings?" Finally it came to me: Our capitol buildings were designed to intimidate. The United States Capitol and many state capitols are modeled after Greek and Roman architecture in neoclassical style. Those Greeks and Romans weren't building malls designed to attract lots of people. They were building temples to the gods. They were designed to inspire awe—and intimidate ordinary people.

Picture the standard capitol. It is usually on a hill, often the highest ground for miles. You walk through meticulously groomed parklike grounds, up a long flight of stairs, through tall stone columns and huge doors into elaborately decorated high-ceilinged rooms.

(If you live in New Jersey, this does not apply. The capitol looks like a seedy store. It's intimidating, but mostly because it looks like a haven for muggers. In Lincoln, Nebraska, where everything is flat, there was no high ground to use. But they did the best they could. The statue of a boy sowing wheat seeds on top of the capitol is the highest point in the Great Plains. In New Mexico, they call it the roundhouse. It is. But I digress.)

Who wouldn't be intimidated? One woman told me she walked into the capitol in Albany, New York, and had to fight off the impulse to kneel and genuflect—she felt as though she had walked into a cathedral. It's easy to be overwhelmed by the hustle and bustle and confusion. I still get lost almost every time I take a group of volunteer lobbyists to the office buildings in Washington.

So, if it's any help, most of us who don't work there every day are in awe of the buildings. The answer is to barge on in, understanding that those are your buildings; you bought and paid for them. When you get in, you will find a lot of friendly people who will help you because they all know the buildings are yours. It won't take long to overcome your fear.

YOUR ATTITUDE ABOUT YOURSELF

Many people say to me, "I'm afraid to talk to a member of Congress. I don't know what to say."

Yes, you do. In education you are the expert. You are the frontline trooper dealing with it every day. You see and live with the results of legislation. You know more than your senator or representative about your building or your school system. And that's all you need to talk to them about—your daily experience.

Many elected officials know nothing about education except their view from their desk as a student. But they want to. Many of them come out of law. Some were journalists. Some have been realtors. They are unlikely to know about the cost of running a bus system, how crowded halls affect behavior, or what it takes to get kids to learn.

This is particularly true for those elected officials who go to Washington and live in an increasingly isolated never-never land. They know it. When you ask them, as I have, they always say the one thing they miss most is the day-to-day contact with real people who can express the real needs of the community. You can fill that void. Your elected official wants to hear from you and you have valuable information to give them.

YOUR ATTITUDE ABOUT YOUR RIGHTS

Maybe it's time to ask a central question: Where do you get the right to lobby? We seem to be a nation of complainers. We take it for granted that we have the right to blame the government for everything and to try to get the government to fix everything.

But step back and think about it for a moment. Where do you get the right to lobby? Most people eventually answer, "It's in the Constitution." Of course. After thinking for a while, you might have said it is in the Bill of Rights, perhaps freedom of speech. Although you are close, it's more specific than that. Remember the First Amendment to the Constitution:

> Congress shall make no law respecting an establishment of religion, or prohibiting the free exercise thereof; or abridging the freedom of speech, or of the press; or the right of the people peaceably to assemble, and to petition the government for a redress of grievances.

Your right to lobby is spelled out in the First Amendment: "to petition the government for a redress of grievances."

You remember from history class how the Bill of Rights—the first ten amendments—came to be written. Our ancestors had just come through a long and bloody war (about eight years) and had created the Articles of Confederation to bring the states together. That didn't work, so they came back and wrote the Constitution. But some states wouldn't sign until they added the Bill of Rights, including the First Amendment.

In that First Amendment, they spelled out your most important rights. It's obvious, given what they had been through, that religion, press, assembly, and speech would merit protection. So why did they put your right to lobby in the First Amendment with freedom of religion, speech, press, and assembly? Because they had not had that right. Historically, the king in England ruled by divine right and could not be questioned. The citizens did not have the right to petition for a redress of grievances. Your ancestors understood that only if the people had the right to complain—constantly—would government have to listen and respond.

This right is one of the founding principles of democracy that separates us from a lot of the rest of the world. This is one reason people from around the world want to come here. It is one reason why I urge you to make lobbying a part of your personal and professional plans and goals.

It is important to understand your key role in making this democracy work by exercising your right to complain. I would even go further. You not only have the right to lobby; it is your obligation, your responsibility. It's important for you to let your government know what you want and don't want. It's a way of repaying those people who, 200 years ago, gave us everything we have today.

It's a way of making sure that those who come behind us enjoy the same privileges we do. When you work through your association on behalf of your special interest, you are not only working for that narrow interest, but you are also making this democracy work the way the founding parents envisioned it.

As I said in the introduction, one of my goals in life is to get all Americans to contact the people they vote for. I am convinced if we can do that, we can solve every problem that faces us. Though I may not be able to get every single American energized enough to write a letter or make a phone call, I hope you will. I hope you will become one of those people who make democracy work. It all starts with your attitude—about politics and politicians and yourself.

Association: Special Interest Groups Make It All Happen

Association = 50% plus one = Success

You can have a powerful influence over elected officials. Particularly when you are talking to the ones you can vote for. But no politician would or should act just because you, or any other one person, have a great idea. They won't because—if they are experienced—they know they only have a certain amount of political capital to spend. They won't waste it on causes they can't win.

Remember the "magic numbers" in our pyramid to power? John McGoughlin, a state representative in North Carolina, explained it this way: "There are lots of good ideas out there. Really good ideas. They are practical. They will work. They will accomplish some useful social goal. But they don't have the political support to go anywhere. At every step in the process you must have 50% plus one or you die."

A nice dose of realism, that. It doesn't matter how righteous your cause is. If you can't show widespread support, your issue will die. And it should. Politics is the art of finding the middle, building consensus, creating a majority. One person's idea, no matter how good it is, will not and should not be given serious consideration just because it's a good idea. Only those ideas that have or reasonably might have or someone can cause to have widespread support are worthy of becoming public policy. Setting majority rule and democracy aside, ideas without widespread support will not work.

The way you demonstrate widespread support is through an organization. Most often political goals are achieved through an association of people, either formal or informal (as in a coalition). If you don't represent something larger than yourself and your good idea, you are unlikely to be taken seriously.

It's like a newspaper op-ed page. I could submit an article outlining a brilliant public health initiative to combat teenage pregnancy. I might get it published as a brief letter to the editor. It wouldn't merit anything more because what I think on that topic, no matter how good the idea, isn't worth much.

If the surgeon general or the chair of a senate committee penned the same article, it could get major play around the country. It would be taken seriously because it would represent some significant constituency, something larger than one person's good idea.

For purposes of this book, we assume that you are a member of an association of school boards, principals, administrators, teachers, or parents. (If you aren't, join now or never complain again.) This usually provides you with the next essential ingredient: the professional lobbyist.

You must have someone on the inside who understands the players and the process and who can lead you through the minefield of legislative deliberation. Think of it in terms of a sports metaphor: The association members are the team. They carry the ball and they score. The professional lobbyist is your coach, providing the experience and judgment to bring your talent and energy to bear in the right place at the right time.

"Professional adviser" usually means a paid lobbyist who is working for you. But I have seen instances where volunteer advocates had the time and knowledge to do the job well. Another possibility is your own elected official. If you can get him interested in your issue, he may be able to help you chart a course through the legislature or Congress.

The keys to success for most associations are (1) get a professional lobbyist and (2) obey him or her. Unless you are focused on politics and your issue 24/7/365, understand the system, know the major players and personalities and understand their motivations, and have the commitment and time to focus virtually all your energy on the political system, you will make costly mistakes. It will take you too long to learn. You may never figure out how to make something happen.

The first time I tried to get some legislation passed was back in the early 1970s, when open meetings and records were a much bigger issue than they are today. Working with Common Cause, a group of us in Atlanta were trying to get the legislature to open the budget process. Our state representative, Sidney Marcus, had agreed to help us. At one point, he told us to pull back because the speaker of the house didn't want this legislation introduced. Sidney said he wouldn't introduce it.

Since we knew the cause was just and right, we decided to pressure Sidney. We started calling him, as his constituents. We decided if we could make his phone ring often enough, we could change his mind. After one or two phone calls, he took his phone off the hook. He didn't want to deal with a bunch of fools—particularly when so many were not even from his district.

Frustrated, we found a freshman representative who agreed to introduce our bill. After he introduced it, in defiance of the speaker of the house, the freshman got squashed and stripped of influence. Sidney, on the other hand, became chairman of a powerful committee.

Later he gave us a lot of help and advice. Because of his position, he was able to help get a lot of our ideas passed into law. Unlike us amateurs, he had enough sense and experience to know what to do and when to do it to get something done. Because we did not factor in Sidney's experience and judgment, we were left holding our ideals, knowing we had gone after the right thing—and had gotten nothing. Be smart. Get a professional lobbyist and follow his directions.

I also draw a distinction between what I call the "inside" (professional) lobbyist and the "outside" (volunteer) lobbyist. You need both. The inside lobbyist is your professional legislative representative. This person knows the ins and outs of the legislature or Congress. He knows the committee system. He knows the players. He knows the arcane parliamentary rules. He knows the secret handshake and the password to get behind closed doors. He could draw a chart showing how a bill moves through the legislature in the dark. It's vital to have a person like this on your side.

But you, the volunteer advocate, the outside lobbyist, don't need any of that. Your skills and value lie in your ability to communicate to the person you vote for and relate your personal experience and your knowledge of how things work in your schools and life back in the district at home.

Professionals provide technical details. They write and edit legislation. They discuss the broad scope and sweep of politics across a nation or state. They use logic, statistics, and politics to persuade. They make the case in general. They develop strategy.

Elected officials want to know three things from you: (1) how an issue affects the people back home, (2) how much the people back home care, and (3) who cares. The bottom line is, no matter how worthy your cause, your elected official wants to know, How many people care, how much do they care, and how many live in my district?

This is information that you can provide better and with more credibility than the professional lobbyist. You work and live with your schools and the people in the district—the professional lobbyist doesn't. You have a critical role in communicating your perspective as an education expert who lives in the district.

All professional lobbyists with whom I have talked (hundreds of them) acknowledge this effect. They will tell you that they can be much more powerful if they have a constituent with them. Much of their power derives from whatever perception the elected official has of the lobbyist's constituency.

There is something else that the professionals can do much better than we volunteer advocates: plan the strategy. They know how to work through the maze. They know about timing and when to compromise—so leave that to them.

I suggest that every organization develop strategies for four time frames that fit within election and legislative cycles. Elections are like tides; they roll in and out very predictably and determine where you put your umbrella and cooler on the beach. Depending on where you are in the cycle, think about

1. From now until election day. What are you going to do in the weeks and months leading up to elections? Depending on your organization's culture, it may range from nothing to running candidates. Just make sure you have considered the election process and have a strategy. This could be a period as long as a year leading up to election day.

2. From election day until the start of the legislative session or Congress. This is when some of your best work can be done. Establish relationships with the newly elected. Strengthen relationships with those reelected. Lay groundwork for your legislative program. Identify key decision makers and legislative gatekeepers. Test your volunteers to see who will deliver.

3. From start of session to end. What will you do in the district? Will you bring people to the capital? What sort of communications system will you use? What's your media strategy? What is the role of your volunteer advocates? Do you have key contacts in targeted districts trained and ready to respond to action alerts? In states that have year-round legislatures, you must have a year-round organization.

4. *The long haul.* It will take years to get what you want, meaning that the immediate success or failure you achieve is not final. You and all with you must be prepared to stick with your issues through defeat and after victory. You must demonstrate a commitment strong enough to convince those in power that you are never going away.

8

Relationship Is Everything

BUILDING THE RELATIONSHIP

I assume that you're working with others in an organization and you want to have an impact on your government. Let's talk about how to build an effective relationship with elected officials so you can make something happen.

You will be better off if you realize that your primary job is building relationships. Issues come and go, and you win some and lose some. But the relationships you build will serve you for a long time, win or lose.

First, realize that most elected officials run for office out of a genuine desire to serve the district they will represent. Even if they run to promote their own agenda or advocate their own issues, they soon learn that unless they are winning friends with service, they won't be in office long. So their driving impulse is to help you if they can. All things being equal, elected officials will try to help you because that's how they get reelected and because that's why they are in office.

The problem is that they can't help all the people who want it. They must carefully choose which issues they get behind to push. A member of Congress told me once that voters have to understand, "We're here to represent you, not advocate for you."

A state legislature might see 5,000 bills introduced in an average year. Anywhere from several hundred to several thousand pass into law. The average representative or senator cannot give careful consideration to more than a handful. She cannot lead the charge on more than one or two. How does she choose? How can you get her to choose to represent your issue? Look at what an elected official's priorities will be on issues.

First, she will try to push the things she believes in, the things that were important in her campaign such as promises made. Most of those will fall by the wayside because they have no support. Issues that win elections often have a hard time finding their way into law. (Your issues are unlikely to have been part of any campaign.)

Second, she will support issues important to leadership. Those who control the house and senate, the governor and president—all have their agenda. Your elected official, the one you vote for, has to work with them to accomplish anything.

It was that consummate legislator, Lyndon Johnson, who said, "If you want to get along, you have to go along." Most legislators, certainly those who are going anywhere, will back leadership because it makes the decision easy. The issues that leadership is backing don't take much time, either. One strategy is for you, your organization, and your professional to get leadership to adopt your issue. This makes for easy sailing but is difficult to make happen.

The third set of issues your legislator will push is in an area where the volunteer advocate plays a key role. These issues are the ones her friends and supporters are interested in and have potential to be passed into law.

An elected official's circle of friends and supporters become her binoculars on the world. They are the filter through which the official sends and receives information and through which she views the world. It's natural enough and we all do it. How much time do you spend listening to people you don't like or don't know or don't agree with?

No matter how hard we try, we all tend to associate with people who are supportive of us and our goals. We tend to reject or screen out our opponents. We tend to ignore people we don't know in favor of those we do. Your challenge is to get into that third set of priorities—friends and supporters. Through your organization, you can get enough other people who are friends and supporters of enough other elected officials to get to the critical 50% plus one.

Remember: Your elected official probably doesn't know anything or care anything about your issue. It may be new or may be something she puts on the way back burner. But if she knows you and cares about you, then she will allocate time and energy to help you. That's what relationship building is all about. If your association has mobilized enough people in this category in the right places in your state or in the nation, you can build up to 50% plus one.

A key question in determining your political success is, How can you get your elected official to care about you? The answer will come as you consider these two questions: (1) What are her personal and political goals? (2) What have you done to help her achieve her goals?

Follow this rule: Never ask a politician for anything until you have helped her enough that she will welcome an opportunity to repay you. If you have done nothing for her, why would she help you, given that she has limited time and there are others with equally worthy goals who have already helped her? What goals of hers might you help get accomplished?

Of course, her first goal is to get reelected. Others might be (1) to pass legislation, either a particular piece or just any bill; (2) achieve recognition (she wants people to know what she has accomplished); (3) advance to a higher political office or to more power in the current office; (4) find new problems to solve; and (5) raise money (see reelection). Each elected official will have a different set of goals. Your job, as a volunteer advocate, is to figure out what she wants and help her get it.

You will stand out immediately from the many people who want something from a politician if you just ask, "What are your goals and how can I help you attain them?" The big number one is reelection. Have you volunteered to work in a campaign? Have you contributed significant money to your PAC or to the election campaign?

If so, you will have access and a warm welcome. But notice, I asked, "Have you contributed significantly?" People frequently ask me how much to give. My rule of thumb is, you want to be in the top tier of contributors. You want your contribution to stand out, whether it is from a PAC or from you personally. Which is another reason why PACs work. They bring together amounts of money that will be remembered.

Contributions are a matter of public record, so find out what others are giving and give enough to stand out. People often tell me they don't feel good about giving campaign contributions. It feels like they are trying to buy a vote. Don't worry. That doesn't happen with legal campaign contributions. For one thing, there are usually limits as to how much you can give. Also, these contributions are on the record and are usually reported in the media.

It frequently happens that your opponents, the people on the other side of your issue, are also giving to the same candidate so the money from opposing sides balances out. Obviously you are giving to promote your cause or interest. So what do you get for the money?

The best reason to give is that you may actually help elect someone who agrees with you. Presumably you are supporting your friends and opposing your enemies. The money you give to a campaign is used to pay for advertising, direct mail, phone bills—the things a person needs to do to get elected. One politician pointed out to me, "You're not giving the money to me; you're giving it to the campaign." It's a good place to start; get "good people" (those who agree with you) in office. It's also true that you cannot expect anyone to be in 100% agreement with you 100% of the time. Just because you help elect someone does not mean she will always be with you.

However, given that most issues could go either way and the republic would survive, and given that most politicians don't know or care about most issues, and given that their basic impulse is to help their friends and supporters, it follows that if you are a significant contributor—either by giving time or money—you get more than access. You get a warm, helping welcome.

I still believe that any citizen with something sensible to say can get a conversation with an elected official, although it may not be easy. It is in the politician's interest to at least listen. (U.S. senators from large states are the exception. Hardly anyone gets to them; they just don't have the time. Getting to their staffers is the key.)

But you want more. You want a relationship with your elected official that moves from professional courtesy to friendly support. You want her wanting to say yes—eager to help. Money isn't the only way. For example, volunteering time to work in a campaign or work on a task force can be even more valuable. This may be hard to believe because of the way television and newspapers portray campaigns. When you see campaigns on television, you usually see the big national races or hotly contested races for the U.S. House or Senate. You see a carefully created picture of crowds of enthusiastic volunteers.

The reality, particularly at the state and local level, is different. The number of consistent volunteers, not paid staff, working in campaigns is very small—usually not even ten in a state race and twenty to thirty in a federal race. One state senator in Michigan told me she had to hire temps, not because she had no supporters but because they were all two-worker families with children and had no time.

You can become a valuable resource just by showing up. Think about the volunteers in Florida who completed the absentee ballot applications for the Republican Party. Think about the people who demonstrated in front of the ballot count in Miami and apparently contributed to getting the count stopped. A small effort by you can make a big difference and will be remembered. You can establish a relationship and you can earn that warm, friendly access by putting out signs, making phone calls, and stuffing envelopes. You can—with relatively little time investment—get on a first-name basis with your elected officials.

It helps to develop a specialty—something you like doing and can do well—that's valuable to a campaign. For example, if you are friendly with numbers and detail, learn how to keep track of campaign contributions and expenses. It's not hard or complicated; it just requires a good eye for detail and a lot of discipline. People who can do this are worth their weight in gold to the campaign and the candidate.

My specialty is signs. When I support candidates, I load up my car with signs. I pull out my special mallet—named Edna—and my heavy-duty staple gun and cruise the precincts I know best, pounding stakes and stapling signs. The mallet is named Edna after Edna Chirico, a county commissioner I supported. I met her one day while I was out riding my bicycle. I saw her putting out signs, talked to her, and asked her what I could do to help. "Put out some of these signs," she said, and I did. Though she's no longer in office, she still remembers me. When she was in office, she would return my calls.

You can be even stronger contributing volunteers as an organization. If your association helps recruit workers, you will get that friendly access. One group I worked with helped set up phone banks for a man running for Congress. For two weeks, they mustered between ten and twenty people every night to make calls around the district. He faced a tough fight in the primary and won by 974 votes. His name was Newt Gingrich. Four years later he was Speaker of the House and he publicly stated that no legislation harmful to this group would pass while he was Speaker. He was as loyal to his friends as they were to him.

One easy thing to do is organize a site visit for your elected official. Let them come to your school or to an association meeting for an appearance. If you put them in front of potential voters, put them in your newsletter, or get media coverage for them, they won't forget.

Once a state senator called and asked me to write a letter to the editor. The newspaper had been covering an issue and he felt he needed to show that his side had some support. It was an issue I cared about, and I was glad to do it. It took me all of thirty minutes to write it and fax it to the newspaper. They published it. Is that senator going to answer my phone call? Will he help me if he can? You bet.

Your elected official needs many things in addition to money and volunteer time. For example, simply knowing what's going on in the community is very important to her. Your contacts at school, church, civic club, and social relationships put you in touch with people and groups of all kinds. Think of the news you hear about a new company coming to town, a new issue some town council is discussing, or something you read in a PTA newsletter. This may be information that doesn't make its way to your elected official. Some districts are huge, especially the congressional districts, and it's difficult for officials to keep up with what's going on.

For example, not too long ago I read in my community newspaper that a small town nearby had formed a task force on education and crowding in the elementary school. Knowing that my county commissioner probably doesn't get that paper, I faxed her a copy of the article. I wrote a note that said, "Here's a meeting you might like to know about. If you can't make it, I can attend and take notes." She faxed me back, thanking me and saying she'd be there and hadn't known about the meeting. It took me five minutes but was most valuable to her. She answers my phone calls and gives me a warm welcome.

This kind of activity is especially helpful in avoiding the "out of sight, out of mind" factor. To build a really good relationship, I recommend you put it on your calendar to make positive contact at least once a month. Stay in front of her with something that helps her so she don't forget. It could be as simple as a letter, a phone call, or a fax, but whatever it is, do something once a month. If you see your elected official is speaking to a group, attend the meeting and shake her hand. Stand up and support her publicly.

It doesn't have to be something that advances your cause—it's better if it doesn't. Just do something to help out or show support. Granted, this may seem simple, but it works—perhaps even more because so few people do it. Most people, if they participate in politics at all beyond complaining, vote and that's all. When you become personally engaged with your elected officials, you stand out like a warm slice of Mom's pound cake.

An example of things few people do is a story about the mayor of the town where I used to live. He and I are in different political parties and we frequently disagreed. But he was a reasonable man and a hard worker. He'd been in office about ten years and had done well by our town in a job that is generally thankless. We were standing out in the street one day, arguing about a zoning issue. Finally, I said, "Okay, Russell, I can see we are never going to agree. But I would like to say one thing. I appreciate the fact that you have served in office and I want to thank you for serving. Even when we disagree, I know you have the town's best interest at heart."

He was shocked. He got a tear in his eye and said, "Joel, in the ten years I've been in office, no one has ever said that to me before." It didn't change his mind. But I'm always thinking about the next time—and he will remember what I said. You will stand out if you do nothing but thank your elected official for serving because so many people never take that simple step.

DYNAMICS OF THE RELATIONSHIP

As I said, the mayor and I are in different political parties, and this is something that comes up often with grassroots volunteer lobbyists. Can I work well with an elected official of a different party—someone whose politics I detest?

I recommend matching grassroots volunteers with elected officials of the same party and outlook where possible. In the best of all worlds, the grassroots contact will be a mirror image of the elected official. But this is seldom possible. Don't worry. When you contact an elected official, she usually won't know what party you are in and won't ask. Even if you are in the other party and she knows it, your issue may not be one supported or opposed by the political parties.

In some states—Pennsylvania and Illinois for example—political party is crucial. In those states your professional adviser will tell you what to do. I do not recommend lying, but neither would I suggest you walk in and announce, "I'm in a different party." If it comes up, be honest.

(Incidentally, saying you voted for her doesn't work. It sounds like you expect something in return. Oddly enough, everyone elected officials meet seems to have voted for them. I used to meet people all the time who would say they voted for me, even though they didn't live in my district.)

No matter what their party, officials know they get elected and reelected by serving people. If they can, they want to help people in their district. It's called constituent service and they know it's what keeps them in office.

As for building a good relationship, I have found it helpful to think in terms of a "favor bank." I have an account with my elected representative just as I have one at the bank, except in this one, I deposit favors. That means you have to look for favors to do. Analyze the person's goals and help her achieve them. You will maintain a good account balance by making regular deposits in the favor bank. Deposit the time you spent putting out signs. Deposit the time you stuffed envelopes. Add to your account when you contribute money.

I think of it as building up equity so I can take out a loan. Who would I like to get favors (or loans) from? In this case, I want something from elected officials. So I want to maintain a favorable balance and never overdraw my account. Before I ask for something, I want to be sure that I have built up favors that will have been remembered.

If this sounds a little too contrived, a little too cynical, remember that this is the way all friendships and relationships work. We just don't usually sit down and analyze it. We aren't methodical about maintaining the favor balance. Like it or not, it will work. My basic rule is, there is only one time you lobby—year in, year out, year round. Never stop. Just like any relationship, there needs to be two-way giving and receiving. If that lapses, where's the relationship?

Many amateurs and newcomers think all they have to do is head off to the legislature while it's in session, make an elegant case, and go home with a victory. It never happens that easily. Politics is a long, messy process. So another important aspect of the relationship is your expectations. You will seldom get everything you want. You must be prepared and committed to the long haul. A major idea—like No Child Left Behind—can easily take between five and eight years to work through.

Your political results will be in direct proportion to your ability to convey the perception that you and your organization are never going to go away. You were here last year, you were here this year, and you will be here next year and the year after. Elected officials are less likely to invest serious time or effort if you do not demonstrate staying power.

There are also limits to what your elected officials can do even when they want to help you. In some legislatures and the Congress, anything that passes depends on a small cadre in leadership. You must get them behind you. There is little or nothing the elected officials who represent you can do by themselves. If leadership in the house or senate is against your issue, accept the fact that you have to convert leadership—no easy task.

Conversely, one of the great strengths of grassroots lobbying is that strong support in the district can allow your elected official to vote in your favor, even when it goes against leadership. Either opposing or not going along with leadership is dangerous. If your elected representatives are going to be effective—for you and others—they must support leadership.

Yet there are times when they don't want to as a matter of personal preference, and times when they don't want to because their constituents are on the other side of an issue. Speaker of the U.S. House of Representatives Tip O'Neill recognized this effect. When he needed to pass a bill he would often have some members who, for one reason or another, needed to vote the other way. O'Neill would sit them all in the front row. If he didn't need their votes, he would let them pass. But if he did, he expected them to vote with him. He would look them in the eye and they would know the moment had come. Can you imagine the pressure?

So if you ask your elected official to go against leadership or to convert leadership, you have to give her a very strong reason. One powerful reason for a legislator to go against leadership, and one that leadership understands, is a strong message from the district. This gives you power because you and your organization can provide that message. Letters, faxes, and other demonstrations of support for an issue from the district give politicians political cover, even to go against leadership. (Another method uses newspaper editorials; more about this later.)

Timing is also important. Legislative affairs run on a schedule. Usually, by the time the session starts, the issue train is leaving the station. You need to get on that train at least six to nine months before the legislature convenes. You need to give your legislator time to absorb your information, check it out, sound out other interested parties, and get back to you. Sometimes your information needs to simmer for a while before it tastes right. You can see the importance of lobbying year in, year out, and year round.

When you do talk with elected officials it is unusual, in my experience, to get a commitment. I mention this because some books advise you never to leave the presence of an elected official without a commitment. All I can say is "Good luck." No smart, experienced elected official will ever give you a commitment until the last possible minute. That's because things can always change.

In one of my seminars, a man told me he had spoken to his representative, had a good conversation, and got a firm commitment. Then the guy voted against him. When questioned about it, the representative answered, "Leadership told me to." I asked the man if this legislator was a first-termer. Yes, he was—as I expected.

An inexperienced politician may make a commitment, only to find

Table 8.1.   Levels of Volunteer Advocate Skills

Rookie	*Pro*	*Hall of Famer*
Make first contact with elected official	Build personal, supportive relationship	Become trusted adviser to elected official
Deliver organization's message	Call, contact, write, fax systematically	Politician and staff call you with requests for information, opinion
Understand need for accuracy	Become trusted information source to politicians	Testify at hearings; talk with media
Respond promptly to action alerts	Report to HQ and discuss results	Gather intelligence, spot trends
Believe lobbying is honorable and effective	Participate in campaigns	Raise money for PAC
Become personally effective	Recruit others to lobby	Organize home-based fund-raisers
Give money to PAC	Politician knows your name, organization, issues	Find allies for coalition
	Give personal money	Write letters to editor, op-ed pieces

good reasons not to keep it. But even if they have to vote against you because of leadership, all is not lost: At least now that politician owes you one.

GAUGE YOUR IMPACT

As you pursue support from politicians, you may begin to see it as a sales process. Scout your prospects, qualify them, build the relationship, respond to objections, and sell the benefits. In sales, you make what is called a "trial close." That is, you check out the prospect to see how you're doing. If you can't get a commitment, you may still be able to get a sense for which way the wind is blowing by asking an open-ended, nonthreatening question such as, How do you feel about what I've said so far? and Is there any other information you need to make a decision? The answers will tell you what to do next.

As you work toward your goal, you will see there is a hierarchy of performance you can achieve. Volunteer lobbyists tend to move through several skill levels as they develop relationships. Let me list those for you now to help you identify your level within the big picture of volunteer lobbyists. It will help you understand more about your job and what you can do, depending on your interest. (See Table 8.1.)

9

Craft a Message to Penetrate
the Clutter Politicians Face

It's time to talk to your elected official and win him over. There are two kinds of messages to get through to your elected official. I call these the "macromessage" and the "micromessage." The macromessage is important to the state (or nation) and is delivered best by the professional lobbyist or leaders of your state or national organization. The micromessage is important to you and me and to the people in your district.

MICROMESSAGE

Your part, as the volunteer advocate, is to help develop and deliver the micromessage to your elected official. In most cases, it works best if the volunteer lobbyist deals only with the micromessage. You are letting your elected official know your issue is important to people in the district. This way you are dealing with things you know well. Indeed, you are an expert; you know things the professional lobbyist doesn't. This approach also means you don't have to know the technicalities of legislation or the legislative process (although that can be useful).

First we'll look at how to construct a message, then how to deliver it. I've surveyed hundreds of state and federal officeholders asking them this question: What do you want from volunteer lobbyists? The answers come back clear and consistent: "Be accurate, be brief, and tell me something new."

Be Accurate

Accuracy means you never go beyond what you know to be absolutely, mathematically true. If you ever knowingly lie, exaggerate, or distort your facts or the other side's position, you are dead. Neither the elected official nor his staff will ever listen to you again. Professional lobbyists know this rule and obey it. Volunteers sometimes don't understand it and get carried away in their enthusiasm. While they don't actually lie, they may not present the whole picture or they may exaggerate. It's easy when you care a lot—but it's fatal.

Fortunately there's an easy way out. Do not go beyond what you know to be absolutely true. Then, if you're doing a good job, you will get a great opportunity—you will be asked a question you cannot answer. And what do you say? "I don't know . . . but I will find out" or, even better, "May I have our professional lobbyist call you?"

The second answer works better because it sets up a warm call between your professional lobbyist and the elected official. You complete an important triangle consisting of the elected official, yourself (the constituent), and the professional. Generally speaking, it's better to leave complicated technical details to the professionals. That's their job; they are likely to have a better grasp of it and they will deliver a consistent message.

Your job is to deliver your part of the message—how the issue affects you, your school, and the people in your community. You want your elected officials to know that you have a headache and what it will take to cure it. You want them to know that your issue, your problem, is important to their voters. If they don't believe the people who put them in office care about the issue, they are free to ignore the professional lobbyist. So impressing upon them that people in the district have a headache is the first step to getting a cure.

Indeed, your own legislator may never need or want to know the details because your solution, your bill or whatever, will be handled in a committee of which he is not a member. But he can be powerful on your behalf conveying his interest to the action committee and leadership.

Your professional lobbyist can present both the larger picture as it relates to public policy and politics and the smaller picture of technical details. Your professional is like a coach, setting game strategy and calling plays from the sideline, but only you and other grassroots activists can carry the ball and score, because only you can make it important to elected officials.

Be Brief

Take no longer than thirty seconds to state what you want and why you want it. If you force yourself to deliver your message in thirty seconds, you will boil it down to its essence. If you can't get his attention in thirty seconds, you probably haven't focused your message.

Often you don't get more than thirty seconds. Politicians are busy and always have a line of people waiting to talk with them. You may run into them at the chamber of commerce or at a party. I've seen more than one very effective communication as a volunteer walked from the elevator to the office with an elected official.

To develop a winning thirty-second message, ask yourself two questions: (1) What do I want? and (2) What key reason can I cite to win support? You want your elected official to support your position. Sometimes you will have a specific bill number. Even when you do, make sure he understands the concepts or fundamental ideas you support because specific bills can change, disappear, and merge. Start with a focused opening that hooks him—it says what you want and why you want it. Use the format: We want . . . because . . .

Imagine we are a group of principals, for example. We want the legislature to allow us to keep our soft drink machines because we use the money to fund extracurricular activities that are really important. Taking away the machines will take away $50,000 a year in activities like chorus, chess club, or debate.

Although it is helpful to give a complete briefing on all aspects of your issue, that isn't usually necessary. Your main goal is to wake up your elected official and let him know that this matters to important people in the district. Give him a sense of what you want and why you want it. Then, if he is still listening, you move to the hardest part of the message.

Tell Me Something New

Unless your representative has just been elected, chances are good that he's heard it all before. There are very few new issues. Anyone who has been in office for a complete election cycle will glaze over the moment your mouth opens unless you can say something he hasn't heard before. You will have to work hard to get him to listen.

In the case of a newly elected person, the challenge is to educate him from ground zero. Most likely, he will be eager to hear you out. In either case, the greater challenge is to cause him to remember and care. You see, the day after the election, they all come down with a disease called TIO: terminal information overload.

They are swamped with issue papers, letters, and personal appeals from everybody with a cause. They get on every mailing list, and at first they try to absorb as much information as possible. They quickly learn—the smart ones at least—that they have to choose very carefully and focus their efforts in order to get anything done. They can't give equal attention to everyone and they can't even give attention to all good causes. They have to pick causes that are important to them and to those who got them elected.

Your job, as a volunteer, is to cut through the clutter with something your official will remember and recognize as important. The antidote for terminal information overload is the anecdote—a story about a living, breathing (or, if it fits, dead) person affected by the issue. It needs to have as much detail as possible to make it credible: names, dates, addresses, ages, occupations—anything that will make the person real.

In the example of the drink machines, tell him how much revenue a single drink machine generates. That's easy to grasp and he probably has no idea. Then give examples of what the revenue supports: trips to regional one-act play festivals, band instruments, whatever.

Share a true personal experience from your own life and schools in his district. In addition to bringing the issue to life, the anecdotes serve another purpose: proving the problem exists. That's important. One of my clients told me about a group of people in Colorado who were trying to get legislation passed to prevent "takings." People in the "takings movement," as it is called, believe the government should not take property or reduce the value of property without fair compensation.

A group in Colorado had introduced its legislation and even gone so far as to get a hearing. When they made their presentation, the first question they were asked was "Can you give us an example that happened in Colorado of a taking such as you oppose?" The spokesmen looked around, paused, scratched their heads—no, they couldn't. They were laughed out of the room. The kind of thing they opposed doesn't happen in Colorado.

I'm told that to this day the lobbyists at the capitol jokingly call out to the lobbyist from the takings group, "Hey, Bob, got your anecdote yet?"

(For several years I told this story in my seminars across the country, based on the story from a client who said he was there. Not long ago, unbeknownst to me, the lobbyist in the story was in my audience. Later he came up and confirmed that it happened just as I had been told, much to his embarrassment. As for his real name, my lips are sealed.)

The real-life stories and anecdotes that illuminate your issue are important for several reasons. If you can't come up with real-life situations, it may look as though you have no problem. The stories dramatize your issue, make it memorable, and give it credibility and cut through the information overload. You take the statistical abstract and turn it into real people.

Politicians are people people. While they are interested in numbers and the broad scope and sweep of things, they respond more to living, breathing people in their district who vote and who they can help. That's why the volunteer's job—your job—is to humanize the issue. To provide the illuminating anecdote that personalizes the issue. To tell the memorable story that will stimulate emotion and action. This is something professional lobbyists often cannot come up with because they don't live with the problem.

For example, banks have fought long and hard for the right to sell insurance. As I worked with a group of bankers to find that illuminating anecdote, most were talking vaguely about helping their customers, having a level playing field, or offering competition to the insurance companies. All this was good, but it was abstract and the same old argument. We couldn't find a way to make it come to life.

Then a woman told this story: "Our bank is in a poor neighborhood. Two times in the last year we have held the accounts for fund-raising drives to pay for funerals for teenagers who were killed. This is a minority neighborhood and funerals are really important. The families had no money to pay for a funeral. Insurance agents don't come to this neighborhood. Since we are already in the neighborhood and have relationships, it would really help these people if we could offer them burial insurance policies." Now that is a compelling story. If I were campaigning to pass a bill to let banks sell insurance, I would put this woman and her story into a video.

I've already mentioned Ralph Wright, former speaker of the Vermont House of Representatives. In his book *All Politics Is Personal* he tells the story of one representative he worked with: "Most of the time he drove me crazy with his 'no-tax, no-spend' votes, but I learned over time I could get him to vote for something if I could place the problem right smack in front of him. I don't mean the issue, rather, the person who would feel the impact of a vote. If I wanted his help on a foster program, for example, I would arrange for him to coincidentally run into a foster kid whom I just happened to have with me. People touched his heart, not theories. Corc [the representative] could be trusted, not if WE believed in the deal, but only if HE believed in it."

When you put real people into a story, you make the case for your issue. You tell them something new. The issue of giving banks the right to sell insurance has been around for many years. There isn't anything new you can say about it.

But you can offer a new story that illuminates the issue in a new way. You can win sympathy and you can get your elected official to remember and care. Make your story as specific as possible. Use real names, dates, and situations. If you've done a good job, the politician may want your help getting in touch with the people involved. Do it. To make your micromessage successful, (1) be accurate, (2) be brief, and (3) tell him something new.

MACROMESSAGE

This is the message you must convey to enough people in the legislature or Congress to get that critical 50% plus one. Usually this will be the result of a thorough deliberative process involving lots of people, lots of fact gathering, and a careful assessment of what is desirable and what is possible. Your association will develop a consensus as to what the macromessage is. Sometimes I call this the "case statement." It spells out the fundamental reasons why politicians should support your cause.

A winning macromessage starts with a firm moral, practical, and political foundation. Without all three parts of this foundation, it's tough to win. The stronger you can make each part, the more likely you are to get what you want. You must demonstrate clearly that your cause is moral, practical, and political. Or at least make it look as moral, practical, and political as possible.

You and I both know there are lots of laws and regulations passed that would fail these tests. Conversely, many ideas people would like to pass into law seem to be good ideas, but they never get anywhere. Much depends on how you "frame" the issue—taking what you have and making it look like what everybody wants. You do it deliberately, step by step, looking for those three elements.

Moral

Is it right? Is it a good thing to do? Is it in the public interest? Can you show that it is? Sure, everybody's for education, but not everybody is for drink machines in schools. You have to make the case. Take, for example, smoking and the regulation of cigarettes.

If you are a cigarette company, you do not argue that cigarettes are good for people. Nobody would buy that. Think for a second: You can't win arguing the health issue. Simply saying, "It's legal," isn't much help, because the response will be "Okay, let's make it illegal." So how can you frame the issue to win?

What do the tobacco companies argue? You've seen the ads. It's not about health; it's about individual rights. You have a right to smoke. You have the right to choose. This is called "framing the issue" and you see it all the time on television. Usually someone will say something like "I'm glad you asked that, Dan, because that's not the issue. The real issue is . . ." Once you frame the issue correctly, it is easier for a politician to support you. Your elected representative cannot argue that cigarettes are healthy. But he can take your side and argue that people have a right to choose.

You and your professional lobbyists must frame the issue in such a way that the politician can take your side and still occupy the moral high ground. The politician needs you to give him that logical framework, that position he can stand on when he answers questions from opponents, family, and the media. You must provide the answer that allows the politician to take your side and be proud and public about it.

Practical

Will it work? If you want to eliminate a regulation or create one, and if you have shown me that it is the right thing to do, you still have to demonstrate to me that it will do the job and be cost effective.

For example, many of my nursing home clients battle with the government every budget cycle to get more money for the Medicaid program. The challenge is to show that it is necessary to put more money in to maintain adequate care for poor people. It's tough because you come very close to saying that if you don't get more money, the quality of care in nursing homes will fall below standards—which no one wants to say.

One strategy we used in Florida was to show—using the government's own numbers—that about half the nursing homes were operating at a loss. We argued that there was no way they could stay in business while operating at a loss and, unless the state wanted to set up its own taxpayer-supported nursing home system, something had to give.

It worked for several reasons. We had credible numbers because the nursing home cost reports are all audited. We could also argue that the alternative would be to set up government nursing homes, which most people understand will be less efficient than those run by private enterprise.

Practicality is important for any issue. If you want to reduce the paperwork involved in making loans, you have to show that the consumer will still be fully informed about interest rates and the real cost of the loan. Got problem with No Child Left Behind? What is it? How big of a problem? How many kids and teachers impacted? How much impact? Want fewer kids per class? Show me how that will make a difference. When you show that your idea will work, then the politician can justify his support. But you must help with that part. It's not your elected official's job to come up with the rationale for what you want.

Political

Does it have—or potentially have—widespread support? Does it serve the public interest or a narrow special interest? In other words, who cares and how much? If you are lobbying an education issue, you can usually make a case that kids will be hurt or helped depending on how the issue turns out. But you will be competing with other ideas and other people who want money for other education purposes and also for noneducation purposes.

Politicians are looking for what's in the public interest. Even if they want to help you, they must be able to make the case that what you want provides the greatest good for the greatest number. They often measure that by how many people they are hearing from and who those people are.

Did you send an e-mail or call? Did you write once or many times? How much you care will be measured in part by the effort you make delivering your message. Were you willing to travel to the capital? If so, that makes a statement about your concern and commitment.

Your politician will ask, "How does this help the average person in my district or this state or the nation? If it doesn't help the average person, whom does it help? How much does it help?" (Remember, who cares and how much?)

As a matter of practical reality, elected officials are only going to put their energy and reputation behind issues that have some chance of winning. They are not in the habit of supporting losing causes, no matter how correct. You must show that they can get the 50% plus one they will need every step of the way and how they are going to get it. So much for the message. Just frame your issue so it looks moral, practical, and political. Be accurate. Be brief. Tell them something new. Then deliver the message.

WHAT WORKS AND WHAT DOESN'T

In our surveys of elected officials, we have asked what are the most effective methods to communicate. Generally they say they would like to have more good communications from constituents, and they have strong feelings about what works best. First, let's look at some things that don't work particularly well.

Petitions

A guy came to my office the other day with a petition. The petition was on its way to Congress. The petition urged members of Congress to allow small businesspeople to fully deduct the cost of health insurance. I think that makes sense and I was happy to sign. I also noticed that this guy worked for an association of small businesses and he now had my address and phone number. Sure enough, he tried to get me to join.

I have no quarrel with what he was doing, although I suspect he was as motivated by a desire to sign up members as he was to fight for the rights of small business. That's because if he had been serious about the issue, he would not have used a petition. Petitions just don't work as a way to influence legislators. I have asked hundreds of politicians and they all confirm: Petitions are next to worthless as an influencing tactic.

Suppose you have 5,000 names on a petition. I'm your senator and you give it to me and say, "Here are 5,000 people who support the idea that small business owners ought to be able to fully deduct the cost of health insurance." I take the petition in my hand. I say, "Thank you."

Then what? What am I supposed to do? Who are these people? Do they vote? Do they live in my district? Are they real? Did they have any clue what they were signing?

I can tell you what your elected official and his staff will say. They think people will sign a petition without reading it. They think that even if the petitioner read it and understood it, merely signing a list does not represent a serious commitment. This is especially true of mass campaigns that sign up people in shopping centers. Therefore politicians pay little or no attention to a petition. A petition with 5,000 names is worth no more than one letter—often less.

If petitions don't work, why do organizations carry on petition campaigns? They do it to enlist, motivate, activate, and energize the people who sign. To get publicity and visibility. Petitions have significant value in recruiting activists, getting public recognition, and other things, but in the battle to influence politicians directly, they are virtually worthless. Remember, politicians suffer from a disease called terminal information overload. They are overwhelmed with input from all kinds of people, and most of it is impersonal and not very thoughtful. It's difficult to imagine anything more impersonal and thoughtless than a petition.

Mass Mail, E-mail, and Telemarketing

In Washington and in your state capital, the political pros distinguish between real communication and fake communication by using the terms "grassroots" and "Astroturf." "Astroturf" is the derogatory term for the mass-generated, impersonal faxes, form letters, and phone calls stimulated by corporations, associations, and their PR firms. An example of this is when some associations hire telemarketing firms in Washington to call their members, give them a quick briefing, then hook them up with a member of Congress.

This can backfire in a big way. When the person in the district talks with a staff member, it only takes a couple of questions to find out that the caller is on the phone because some hired agency in Washington called. The caller really doesn't know much about the issue. It's embarrassing to the person and to the staff member. Staff reacts negatively because they have wasted their time.

The same thing is true with computer-generated faxes and letters. The staff who receive them quickly detect that the message is from a computer, not a person. They not only discount it but get angry because they have to deal with what is essentially meaningless communication. Some associations set up e-mail communications and telephones at their conventions. They rope in people and tell them who to write and what to write. The phone calls, faxes, and e-mails pour into Washington.

In Washington they say, "Oh, yeah, more mail from the convention." They answer it, usually, but what effect do you think it has? It's similar to what one politician described. He said he could always tell when a preacher has stirred his flock because on Wednesday he will get a load of mail. Although he answers it politely, he doesn't think there's much commitment there and it doesn't sway him.

If these techniques don't work, why do people use them? Several realities drive this sometimes counterproductive activity: Organizations need to show their stakeholders they are doing something and it's an easy way to get people involved. The preachers need to stir up their flock and help them feel they are doing something. It's easy. The companies providing these services do a good job of selling and professional lobbyists are all looking for an easy way to get influence. The folks involved are fooled into believing they have had significant input. (This may lead to frustration when it doesn't work.)

Exceptions to the Rule

There are instances in which an overwhelming number of people participate and the pressure is too intense to resist, even though the commitment is shallow. In one famous case, Congress wanted to take quarterly tax deductions from savings accounts. The banks got millions of customers to send in preprinted cards. It worked.

If you shoot enough BBs at a brick wall, you can eventually break it down. But it takes a lot of BBs. Only a few issues and a few organizations are capable of stimulating that kind of response and they can't do it often.

It's also true that everything and anything you do has some impact. It is also true that you can, with enough effort and the right techniques, stir up meaningful communication. If you can cause constituents to have thoughtful, personal communication with the person they vote for, it will work. But most massive efforts produce only shallow, hit-or-miss letters and phone calls with little result. All I can say is, every member of Congress or state legislature and every staff person I have talked with, hundreds of them, say these mass techniques have little or no positive effect and often have negative effect. I believe in using techniques that we know will have a strong impact.

GETTING PERSONAL

So what do elected officials and their staffs want? Thoughtful, personal communications from people who can help them get reelected. Something that shows a real person in the district cares. They want to know who cares and how much. Show you care about them, you care about your issue, and you care a lot.

Letters

Politicians tell me—and numerous scientific surveys show—that personal contact, for example, through letters and phone calls, is the most powerful contact. After face-to-face, I give the edge to postal letters, especially at the state level. As for Congress, because of the ricin poison and anthrax scares, postal mail can take forever to arrive. When it does get there, one chief of staff told me, it is often "fried," that is, brittle, because it has been treated to kill anything in it.

Unless you hand carry your mail, it's problematic. In the near future I expect that everything sent will be scanned into electronic form and forwarded to Congress, so postal mail has significant limitations. That makes e-mail and faxes your best options.

Historically, it's surprising how many politicians use very similar words when they answer the question, "What is the most powerful communication, the one you are most likely to respond to?" Their reply is usually, "A letter written on ruled paper in pencil by a little old lady."

I don't suggest you do that because it might come across as phony. (On the other hand, it would stand out. For example, handwritten thank-you notes have enormous penetrating power.) But the old-lady letter symbolizes what they are looking for: a real person with a real problem who cares a lot and lives in the district. A person who sits down to write a letter is expressing a serious commitment. It takes longer to write a letter than make a phone call. Few people send a thoughtful, personal letter, so they stand out when they arrive.

For years, I have given the same advice: Make your letter one page, one issue. Just tell the politicians what you want and why you want it. However, as I continue probing to find what works best, I get more examples convincing me that a thoughtful, personal, really good, long letter will get really good, long consideration. Staff and elected officials alike have cited examples of single letters that were so compelling they had to hold a meeting to answer them. The letter raised good issues and made them think.

Once I was standing with a group of people in Austin talking to State Representative Patricia Grey in her office when she noticed a name tag. She said, "You sent me a letter, didn't you. [The wearer nodded yes.] I haven't responded yet because it was such a good letter I haven't had time to think through my response." She said the letter raised so many questions that she had been thinking and researching for two weeks to answer him. That's powerful. That kind of consideration is about as good as it gets. (Their exchange of letters is on pages 207–209.)

A long, thoughtful letter carries a heavy weight of commitment that must be answered. It also stands out because almost all others are short. But it must be a good letter, full of facts and persuasive argument and meaningful detail from the politician's district or state.

Some kinds of letters don't work, however. If you get an action alert from your association or company, personalize it into your own words on your own letterhead, using your own examples. Many groups nowadays send out talking points and ask you to select your own and rewrite them. That's a good idea.

Some people take an action alert or sample form letter, write their legislator's name at the top and put their name at the bottom and send it. Don't laugh—I have seen letters that arrived in Washington with a computer code salutation (Name) (Address) (City) (State) (Zip) crossed out and the recipient's name written in. At the bottom, still shining through the ink, were the words (Your Signature), dutifully crossed out with a real signature nearby. Needless to say, that doesn't meet the standard for thoughtful, personal communication.

Some people use preprinted postcards that way. Sign your name and drop it in the mailbox. I'm not saying it has no effect. Enough postcards at least indicate that the issue has a constituency willing to sign a postcard. It may get some attention. It only works if you can produce tens of thousands of those and most of us aren't usually engaged in a mass campaign that can produce those kinds of numbers.

What works is a personal, thoughtful communication from a constituent. Your letter can be as simple as three paragraphs: (1) Tell your politician what you want, (2) cite an example from the district, and (3) say you'll check back in two weeks.

Will you get a form letter back? Probably. That's okay—particularly if it seems supportive. If you get a letter back that is so vague it gives you no clue, here's a secret: Send another letter; only this time, in the last paragraph, ask a question he cannot answer in a form letter. Keep it up until you get an answer. It may take awhile and a phone call. Sometimes a politician is trying not to state a position or give you an answer.

At the very least, you will make some staff person think through and perhaps have a discussion with a more senior person. Getting them to construct the form letter is a good first step toward winning support. The presence of a specific form letter is a sure sign they are hearing from the district. (Their form letter to you is good. Your form letter to them is bad.)

Here's another secret for a powerful letter and especially an e-mail. Begin your letter by accurately stating the number of the district you live in. (You have a numbered district for your state senate and for both the state and federal house of representatives. For United States senators, indicate your state by your address.) When you do this, you automatically lift yourself out of the pack of passionate but uninformed constituents.

You show you are politically savvy and a serious player. Not one voter in 10,000 knows the number of the district they live in, even among those who know the name of their representative (and that's a very small group too). Believe me, those elected officials know their district number and will respect you when you speak their language.

Another tip. When you send your letter, make sure to give them permission to call you late at night or on the weekend and include your number at home—particularly if your politician is in session. Elected officials work long days; often the only time they have to call is on weekends and at night. Your willingness to do this not only makes their lives easier, but it also shows that you are committed beyond normal working hours. If you have a private number or cell phone number, give it to them and tell them that's what it is.

Faxes

Faxes work about as well as letters, and they are faster and easier. The only downside is the quality depends on the printer where they arrive and they will be in black and white, whereas your letterhead, particularly if you are writing on company letterhead, my have more impact because it is in color. Elected officials tell me they like faxes because they are easy to work with. They often just write a note on them and fax them back.

One thing that seems to work well is to send something timely from the newspaper with a note on it. Chances are good you will get there before the papers do and your note takes on added value. You are helping them and they will remember you.

When you send a fax, send it to the right person by name. Usually this will be the person handling education issues. Then call to make sure he got it. Congressional offices are not always the most organized places and paperwork gets mislaid a lot. Sometimes faxes don't arrive because of technical problems and sometimes they just get lost. The person you are sending to may be gone. Your follow-up call gives two impressions and doubles the chance that the right person will see it.

Almost every computer in operation today has the ability to send a fax straight out of your word processor. Usually this works by hitting the print button and choosing fax as the printer. This allows you to easily create a personal letterhead if, for example, you don't want to use your office letterhead in a political letter. Because it comes straight out of your computer, it gives the best possible quality coming out of the fax.

When I send letters like this, I sign my name using a script font in 24-point type. It looks like this:

Joel Blackwell

Phone

Legislators love the phone because they can have a quick two-way dialogue. But it's often hard to get them during office hours. If you call, it helps to make notes about what you want to say before you call. Here's a checklist for your lobbying phone call.

1. Primary objective. What do I want to happen?
2. Secondary objective. What will I settle for?
3. What points am I going to make to get the results I want?
4. What open-ended questions can I ask to keep the conversation going?
5. What exact words will I use (write them down) to ask for what I want?
6. What is the likely response when I close by asking for what I want and how do I respond?

One thing I observe when I watch people make phone calls is that they often get nervous and talk too fast. You don't have the advantage of using your own body language or reading theirs, so slow down. Speak distinctly. Make sure they know who you are not only by giving your name slowly and clearly, but also by anchoring them with an image they will remember: "We talked at the chamber meeting in April" or "I sent the article on taxes two weeks ago." They get so many calls that if they don't know you like a family member they may not understand who you are.

If you make your pitch and he isn't asking questions, get off the line—you haven't engaged him. Follow up with an e-mail or fax. Reiterate what you meant to say and what you thought you heard in response. Many times you will get voice mail and need to leave a message. I love voice mail because I've got my message ready and can be pretty sure I have their attention for thirty seconds until I leave the number.

I state my name and phone number v-e-r-y slowly at the end of my message and then repeat it. It is amazing how many people compliment me on this. In contrast, I have gotten many voice mails where the caller, so used to leaving his own number, speeds up and leaves something I can barely understand. So make sure you give your name and number carefully and slowly. You want your politician to call back.

What About E-mail?

Especially since the anthrax and ricin scares, a lot of people are using e-mail. What staff and politicians say is that they get it and read it, and they like the ease of response, but they discount it compared to hard copy mail. I think that's because it looks and feels transient. It lacks permanence. The volume of e-mail is increasing to the point where much of it passes untouched by human hand and barely scanned by human eye. By one estimate from the Congressional Management Foundation, in 2004 the House of Representatives alone received more than 99 million e-mails. There is no way to give consideration to that many messages.

Others conclude the same thing. An article in the *Washington Post* by John Schwartz was headlined, "Sometimes E-mail Just Doesn't Deliver." Schwartz quoted activist Jonah Seiger, who works for a consulting firm called Mindshare Internet Campaigns: To make an impression in a legislator's office, "it is very important to make noise. E-mail doesn't do that." Electronic mail, Seiger said, "has no weight. It has no mass. It comes in quietly and gets filtered by computers."

American University and Bonner Associates in mid-1998 did a study on e-mail and found that it is substantially discounted. One flaw that staff people cite about e-mail is that e-mail addresses don't tell where a person lives. A majority of staffers I talk to disregard e-mail—delete it or send a bland automatic response—unless they have some clear indication the person lives in the district. One politician recently told me he never responds to e-mail. "If I do, they send me another note. I respond again. They respond again. It never ends. So I just send a letter and that's it. That's all I have time for."

But this is changing rapidly and e-mail is clearly the wave of the future.

It just works too well. When you are using e-mail, it is even more important to signal in the subject line that you live in the district. Something like "Message From Joel Blackwell in Arlington." Give your name, town, and address right up front of the message so they can screen it in.

Sending a message from your association's website usually works best because this allows the association to track it. However you communicate, make sure the association gets a copy of your message and the response. You can also send messages from your member of Congress's website, but make sure your association gets a copy.

PREPARING FOR PERSON-TO-PERSON COMMUNICATION

While I am a great believer in letters, nothing beats an eyeball-to-eyeball conversation. Politicians often tell me, "It's hard to say no when you're looking them in the eye."

Before you have an oral communication—in person or by phone—I recommend you take out a 4 x 6 card. Write down specifically what you want to happen, for example, "I want you to vote for House Bill X." Give three good reasons why your elected representative should support it. Three ways it will make a difference in the district. Write down an example of how it's working, or not working, or will work. This example should be concrete, specific, and about a specific person that you can name (the anecdote).

For example, I was working with convenience store operators who wanted to pass a state law requiring mandatory ID checks for the age of any person buying tobacco products. There was a law in place making it illegal to sell tobacco products to anyone under eighteen. But it was often ignored. The police had just run a sting operation in which they dressed up a mature looking sixteen-year-old girl and sent her around to buy cigarettes—which she did. Then they arrested the clerks.

I felt the store owners could make a good case that it was unrealistic to ask minimum wage clerks to be the enforcers and to make the decision who to ask. It was especially unfair to punish them for what could be an honest mistake. It would be much easier to make everyone show an ID.

When trying to convince a politician, my rule is to focus on the people affected by the issue. In this case, that meant I had to tell the story of the clerks, bring them to life not as bad, uncaring people, but as mostly young, not very well educated low-wage earners struggling to get by, often rushed, worried about their families, facing a line of people—all in a hurry—wanting to serve them, to do a good job. They don't want to get into an argument. It's easier for them to just sell the cigarettes instead of asking for ID. I had to talk about the sting and ask the question, "What good did it do anyone to lock up a clerk or fine them?"

Then I proposed an easier, better way to keep tobacco products from the kids. Make everybody show an ID. Put the burden on the buyer. If kids are faking their age, arrest them, not the clerk. You will always make your case more powerful when you show a politician a real problem affecting real people in their district and give them a solution. Be accurate. Be brief. Tell them something new.

MEETING WITH YOUR REPRESENTATIVE

1. When meeting with your representative, be clear in your own mind about what you want to achieve. Usually you will be visiting as part of a coordinated effort through your association. You will have an issue and information about the issue to bring to their attention. Your association should have given you a specific assignment such as to present information and ask for a response or ask for support of a particular bill or concept. Get your targeted elected official to contact another elected official and ask for action, such as a vote in committee. Become a cosponsor.

If you cannot say precisely what you want from this meeting, ask the question: Why are we doing this? If you cannot come up with an answer, maybe you shouldn't have a meeting.

2. Make an appointment. If your appointment has been made by the association, confirm it. If not, call the office where you are meeting, and ask for the appointments secretary or scheduler. She may want to know in detail what you want to talk about, so be prepared to explain. Think of it as practice pitching your story. It's okay to lay your cards on the table early, since no one in politics likes surprises.

3. When you get an appointment, follow up with a confirmation letter and send a copy to headquarters.

4. Inform yourself before the meeting. Gather biographical information on your targeted elected official. The more you know about the person, the better you can relate to him. Association staff may provide you with extensive, detailed information. If you haven't received it, ask for it. You can usually get a lot from the Internet, either from the elected official's site, newspaper archives, or just a general search. It's a good idea to learn to do this on your own and to keep an eye out for information on TV and in newspapers back home. You only have one or two politicians to track and your association staff has to monitor the whole Congress. Get names of staffers you may encounter, their job titles and backgrounds. Get directions to the office and the office phone number in case you get lost. Make sure someone in your party has a cell phone.

5. Help the elected official and staff prepare for your meeting. Call and ask who is handling your issue. Send information that supports your case, as much as you wish, with an executive summary no longer than one page. (A staffer told me no one in Washington had read anything longer than one page since the typewriter was invented.) State what you want, why you want it, and what it means to the district and to you personally. In a follow-up call, ask if they need any more information and give them permission to call you anytime at home or at the office.

6. Prepare yourself. Get your organization's issue paper and review it. However, keep in mind that nobody expects you to be an expert on legislation. Your job is to be the expert on your little piece of the issue as it affects you. If you can give the broader picture, that helps. But your priority is to tell your elected representative how your issue plays out in the district, in your school, and in your life. You are an expert on what's going on in your own life and school and that's what they need to hear from you.

7. Find out what position your targeted senator or representative has taken on your issue in the past.

8. Find out what the next step is in the legislative process (introduce the bill, committee hearing, markup, and so forth). Your professional lobbyist will know. Your targeted elected official may not know where your issue is in the legislative treadmill, and he will probably ask you. You can also avoid the embarrassment of learning that your bill has already been passed or defeated.

9. Take an index card and write down what you want from the elected official, as specifically as possible. Put down three or four reasons why the issue is important in the district and in your school. What is happening or will happen to real people in a general sense? Picture a specific person who is being or will be affected. Jot down key words to remind yourself how this person will be affected. Be able to make this person come alive with a name, age, job, address, and so on. The story about a real person will be what they remember most of the time.

10. Get ready for culture shock. The staff you will encounter in the legislature and Congress may be younger than you and of a different outlook and ethnic background than the people you normally deal with. Especially in Washington, you may find yourself sitting down with a twenty-something wearing baggy clothes who looks too young to be dealing with weighty matters. Avoid displaying shock or commenting on her age. (One of my clients came out of a series of meetings and said, "My God, the country is being run by children." It's true.) Regardless of her youth and inexperience, this person is in a position to help or hurt you. Speak with respect in a businesslike manner.

11. Take two other people. Although there may be internal reasons that force you to take more or less, taking too many people is the most common mistake people make, according to staff and elected officials. (I have had some express surprise that so many people came all this way, so maybe numbers do count sometimes.) Among other things, you will often be in a tiny, cramped space that has difficulty accommodating even three, especially in state offices. No matter how many you have, assign the following functions. (1) Key contact: delivers the message and asks for help. Does most of the talking, working from 4 x 6 card or other notes. Keeps conversation on track and focuses on purpose of meeting. Has practiced and rehearsed the message. Stays on message and gets back on message. (2) Secretary: handles papers, hands over background material as needed, gives a list of volunteer advocates who are present with names, employer (if relevant), mailing address (home), and phone numbers. Business cards are okay, but put your home phone number on them. If you use business cards, gather them before the meeting and hand them over in one stack all at once (no fumbling through purses and billfolds). (3) Observer: takes notes of what is said, any requests for more information, promises made. If the staffer says she will get back, ask when and let her know you are writing it down. You have a right to expect a prompt follow-up. Good notes equal power. Don't worry that staff will feel offended somehow.

This is a business meeting. If you feel the need to explain, just say, "We want to make sure we follow up on everything."

Look at body language and facial expressions of the targeted elected official and staff. Are they fidgeting, looking at watches, answering the phone? Are they merely polite or genuinely interested? Was the meeting ended with a preplanned interruption? What was the tone of the meeting? These things may tell you more than the words spoken.

Watch to see if the listener really understands what is being said. It's okay to interrupt and suggest going back over something to make sure it is clear. Notice what kind of notes the staff and/or elected official are taking. Some are compulsive and take reams of notes. It always concerns me that they may not be listening, that perhaps the note taking is for show. So I like to let them know up front that we will be giving them complete written information on everything we have to say. Frankly, I would rather have them listening and not taking so many notes.

I was once with a lawn-care group talking to a member of Congress when they delivered what for them was a central article of faith about chemicals on lawns: "The dose is the poison." To the people in the industry, this was like saying "Do unto others . . ."

But the congressman, Eric Fingerhut from Ohio, didn't move. I interrupted and said, "Congressman, they just said something important and I wonder if they made it clear?" He said he didn't know what it meant. We were able to back up and run it by him again with explanation. At the end of the meeting he had the central points we had come there to make.

12. At the meeting, take care of business. This is not a social gathering—it's a business meeting, very much like a sales call. While you don't want to be brusque, you do want to use your limited time well, which is another reason to keep the group small: Introductions take a long time and everyone may feel they have to chat. While you want to follow the lead of the person you are talking with, remember you have a purpose and an agenda. Say hello, give a brief introduction and a list of who is there with biographical information, and get to work. State what you want and why you want it.

13. When you get a signal that your time is up, say, "Let me check my notes to make sure I said everything I came here to say." Then pause carefully. Look at your 4 x 6 card and think—Did I ask for what I wanted?—just to make sure you haven't missed anything. If you need to, restate your position and ask for what you want.

14. Ask the staffer something like this: "When will you speak to the Representative Smith and let him know what we said?" You might give the staffer a personal note with your home phone number and say, "Will you give this to him (or her)? Since we haven't been able to talk in person, I would like to talk by phone." Remember, one of the jobs of staff is to screen out people, to protect the elected official's time. You need to be assertive in showing that you want to speak with your elected official, if not now, then soon. I have had staffers tell me that sometimes they just take information and file it away. This is not what you want.

15. Follow up. Send a note of thanks to all concerned, including the relevant staff, receptionists, and so on. Briefly reiterate what you and your observer heard in the way of results. Thank them for support or urge reconsideration as appropriate and assure them that any promised follow-up will be coming soon.

16. Call or send a report to your association headquarters. This increases the value of your meeting many times and helps your lobbyist plan strategy.

Two tips: First, never threaten or use language that can be interpreted as threatening. Statements such as "We helped you get elected last time," "We have a lot of voters in our organization," or "This will get a lot of votes" will make your politician defensive and turn him off immediately. Anyone in office already knows the political reality. Not only is it unnecessary, but it will also be regarded as crude, rude, and amateurish. If you have the power to intimidate, you do not need to say so—your politician already knows it. If you don't have it, you will look foolish.

Second, communicate with a purpose. Some people call or write so often and about so many topics they are considered slightly daffy and lonely. "Don't be a pen pal," said one staffer. Writing about every topic that strikes your fancy will turn you into a pen pal wannabe. These letters are considered pitiful and irritating.

I am often asked how many times you can communicate. I think as long as you have something new to say, it's okay. But just repeating the same stuff quickly becomes an irritating nag and is counterproductive. My gut feeling is that you need to be in front of staff and politicians with something useful and/or helpful or in person four to six times a year just to be remembered.

BECOME A HUMAN

One of the most effective leave-behinds I've seen was created by Chuck Johnson of Farwell, Michigan. Chuck is an avid motorcyclist. He had been trying to get to see Senator Debbie Stabenow without success. He thought it might be that she didn't have time to talk with a "biker." Motorcyclists have an image problem with people and politicians who don't know them. So Chuck created on his computer and brought to Washington an 8½ x 11 bound booklet to leave with members of Congress. It contained his résumé and color photos.

The first page told about him in considerable detail in résumé format. Then he had pictures of his wife, a Methodist minister, in her clerical robes standing beside the church sign. Pictures of him on his motorcycle, with his grandchildren, and finally of him on the motorcycle in a parade with a huge yellow man-size chicken character on the back, the sort of mascot you see at a football game. The parade pictured kicks off an annual chicken barbecue in Farwell.

Chuck reports that a staffer gave this handout to the senator, probably with some amazement. Senator Stabenow thumbed through and realized that she had walked in that parade and seen the chicken character and Chuck. She got in touch with him and he was finally able to talk with her. He had made a personal connection.

I don't know what's going to work for you. But I do know it is important that you become something more than just a title or a business card. Some people do this well just by telling about themselves. The important step is to help the people you talk with remember you as a multidimensional person who is part of the community.

You're not just a principal or superintendent or school board member. You have family, activities, and other connections that make you part of the community. In explaining this, you may find some common bond with the person you are talking with. At the very least, you become more memorable.

Media Lobbying: Using Editorial
Pages to Influence Politicians

MEDIA LOBBYING: LOW RISK, LOW COST, HIGH PAYOFF

Although television is more powerful than newspapers, when it comes to moving the masses, and moving politicians, newspapers still set the public agenda. Did you notice in the list of powerful influencers in chapter 5, six of the top ten were newspapers?

This may be because the printed word, particularly in politics, has more credibility. Decision makers understand that television contains more entertainment than information. I'm talking about using news media to directly influence political decision makers, and there newspapers carry more weight. For one thing, television suffers because it only has one "page" and everything appears equal on that page. Sitcoms, commercials, and news are all mixed up together. And nowadays, even more than newspapers, television doesn't cover the substance of politics and policy.

While newspapers take editorial stands every day that represent the stand of the newspaper, very few television stations offer an institutional opinion or urge action. You do get shades of opinion on Fox network and some others and some radio talk show hosts have an influence. Whether they would ever feature your issue is an open question. But even if you get on, I'm not sure how much these shows influence politicians. I am sure, and the politicians and staff tell me, that newspapers back home are very influential.

An editorial can urge legislators and citizens to support your position. Huge numbers of opinion leaders look to the editorial page for guidance because they don't have time to analyze issues themselves. Though few politicians will admit it, they also watch editorials to get a sense of which way the wind is blowing.

Those of us dealing with education issues often find that it is difficult to get on TV or get enough time to explain complicated issues. Television wants sound bites and few things in education can be explained in five or ten seconds. Also, when you are campaigning for an issue and trying to move Congress or a legislature, it's easier to cover the whole state or nation through newspapers. In almost every market an editorial in a single daily paper will reach most of the decision-making population and all the political leadership. You can target single districts through the small dailies and weeklies with enormous impact.

Newspapers also have another advantage: permanence and ease of handling (compared to videos or television). You can tear out an editorial and mail it to elected officials, but it's hard to get them to watch a video.

Take another look at the list of influencers mentioned earlier in "Fighting for Education":

1. Face-to-face conversation with constituent
2. Letter, fax, or e-mail from constituent
3. Phone call from constituent
4. National daily newspaper article
5. National daily newspaper editorial
6. District daily newspaper article
7. District daily newspaper editorial
8. Orchestrated mail from constituents
9. Op-ed opinion pieces in major daily newspapers
10. Op-ed opinion pieces in local daily newspapers

Six of the top ten influencers are newspapers. Four of the six are editorial pages. If you aren't using newspaper articles and editorial pages, you are missing six of the top ten influencers. It's easy to see how it works when you think about what motivates people in office or who want to be in office.

Imagine that you are an elected official. You pick up your hometown newspaper and read an editorial explaining why you should vote a certain way on a particular issue. Does it have any impact? You bet—but not because the logic of the editorial is so persuasive that politicians read it and change their minds. It's more complex than that. When it comes to politics, one of the ways associations demonstrate clout is through their ability to capture headlines and airtime.

If you can create coverage and focus editorial opinion, you demonstrate that you are a force to be reckoned with. You gain credibility. Politicians must respond to what the media says is important. If the media says your issue is important, it is. If you train people how to talk with newspaper editorial boards and to follow up, you can get

1. A significant number of positive editorials
2. Increased political support because newspaper support gives neutrals permission to take your side
3. Better understanding of your issues by journalists and hence more positive coverage
4. New members working for the association
5. Increased and improved television coverage
6. More, and more effective, letters from supporters to politicians
7. In the case of associations, members who have a heightened perception of the value of membership (you have given them something they seldom see—support in the media)

MEDIA LOBBYING

If you want to be effective in projecting political power, establish a network of media-savvy members or employees just as you have key contacts to contact politicians. They can be the same people. Just as you have (or hope to have) a person assigned to targeted members of the House and Senate, state and federal, have one for each daily newspaper and TV station.

Many in association leadership worry about giving that kind of responsibility to rank-and-file members. My experience shows that with training, you can multiply your effectiveness many times at no risk. A good place to start is getting your advocates to ask for editorials. Many times you will find that school board members, principals, and other administrators already have good newsroom contacts; they just aren't aware they can use editorial pages to achieve legislative goals.

You will have to reassure them that talking to editorial writers is not the same as being interviewed by reporters who are often in an adversarial state of mind. Editorial writers are usually friendly and eager to hear you out. The atmosphere is more relaxed, more like a discussion than an interrogation with a reporter. Since you initiate the contact, you are prepared and you control the message. Here's how you can recruit and train your members to ask for newspaper editorials and then use the editorials.

Getting Started

First, coordinate with your professional lobbyist. He or she needs to have input and veto power over this and all public relations techniques. Only use grassroots lobbying and public relations when the professional lobbyist agrees it is appropriate.

Second, select editorial markets. Do you want to aim at all major markets in the state or nation? You may be able to get more bang for your buck targeting key districts. Remember, politicians are your real targets and the most powerful ones often live in out-of-the-way places, outside major media markets.

Each market usually has only one daily newspaper, but a member of Congress may have more that are important. One member I interviewed said the people in his district read newspapers from three states because his district borders two other states.

Once you've identified your target newspapers, call and say you want to talk to the editorial writers and present an idea. They will tell you what the process is to get on the agenda.

When dealing with a large paper, you might speak to an editorial board of five or ten people. Sometimes a large newspaper's board will have such a crowded agenda they will ask you to speak to a single writer who specializes in education. This can work in your favor because a specialist is well informed. This one person may determine a paper's stand. In smaller papers, one person may write all the editorials, so that's who you talk to.

Timing is important. Editors want a timely event to write about. They want their editorial to be "newsy." So if you can get to them with your request for an editorial three to four weeks before a key event, such as a committee hearing or vote, it gives them a reason to write the editorial "news hook."

While it's okay to brief them anytime, they usually want to wait until there is some reason to publish the editorial. You'll get the best results when you give them your briefing three to four weeks ahead of some newsworthy event such as the introduction of your bill, a hearing, or a news conference. (Sometimes you have to create the newsworthy event.)

Who Should Go to the Newspaper?

Editorial board members tell me the most common mistake is to bring too many people. Three people works best: one expert from the association and two members who live or work in the newspaper's community. Newspaper editors are like politicians; they want to talk to their constituents about real people and real problems such as schools in their circulation area.

Given the makeup of most newsrooms, sending white, middle-aged men in pinstripe suits may work against you. I try to select a mix based on gender, age, and race or ethnic background. Many times, editors have commented privately to me that it is refreshing to talk with a business group that is "diverse." What they mean is something other than middle-aged white guys in suits.

Advance Materials for the Newspaper

Often editorial writers ask for material to read before the meeting. Send as much as you wish but don't be surprised if they have not read it when you get there. I remember one session I had arranged at the *Orlando Sentinel,* a major paper in a major state—Florida. I had been talking with the editorial page editors for weeks. I had sent two different sets of materials in advance. I had briefed them on who would be coming and what we wanted to talk about. Everything was set.

When I got there with my group, someone I didn't know greeted us and said, "The person you were supposed to talk with had to leave. I don't know who you are or what you want, but come on in and tell us." (I'm not complaining. We got a supportive editorial.)

Materials

Take a one-page outline that states clearly what you want: "We hope you will write an editorial urging a change in how schools' test results are evaluated . . ." Spell out three to five major supporting reasons in one short sentence each. On a separate sheet, elaborate supporting facts and figures in one paragraph for each reason. Make it two pages or less. This gives them a one-page summary of what you want and why it's a good idea, then two more pages of elaboration. They can get the whole picture in three pages.

As you think about what to give them, remember that the typical editorial is no more than six to eight inches long, often shorter. What they ultimately write will be brief and to the point, so look at their editorial page and give them something that fits in their format.

Naturally they like to go through a more exhaustive process to reach the conclusions in that short editorial. They have to justify their opinion. Add any documents, articles, or other data, especially from independent sources, to help your case. Charts, graphs, and photographs enhance your chances of being understood and getting an editorial.

Improve your credibility by providing a list of names and phone numbers of others who are well informed on the issue, especially including the opposition. (You don't have to give them the most articulate, forceful opponent.) Use people local to the newspaper whenever possible. Give names, titles, expertise, and phone and fax numbers to make it easy to contact them.

Making Your Case

Be able to tell them what difference it makes to people in their community: What is the impact in the circulation area of this newspaper? How many students and schools or teachers and principals will be affected? How much money is at stake? Use specific numbers and local examples.

Appearance Counts

Keep everything simple. Fancy presentation folders and four-color brochures smack of "slick" and "rich." Plain white typing paper, stapled together, works fine. Have enough copies for everyone plus extras.

Although you need to take handouts, I advise you to hold them until the formal presentation is finished to ensure the editors are listening instead of reading. I can promise that if you give them handouts early, the editors will read them and will miss part of what you say.

Consider the editor's reaction to clothes, expensive jewelry you wear, and car you drive (sometimes they will walk you back to the car). Dress code in most newsrooms is college campus 1968. You may get a negative reaction if your group looks like dress-for-success clones.

The volunteer president of one group I worked with had started with almost nothing and worked his way up to become the owner of a successful group of nursing homes. He drove a Jaguar and wore a diamond-studded Rolex. We had a vigorous discussion about the watch. I explained that we were going into editorial boards asking for the state to provide more money for Medicaid, a program for poor people. A great many people perceived that much of this money would create profit for nursing homes. I tried to explain that it could create skepticism to be asking for more money to run the nursing homes while wearing a $10,000 watch. From his point of view, he had worked hard to earn the watch. He was willing to tell anyone who had questions exactly how hard he had worked to earn that watch and what it meant to him.

The problem is, newspaper people often are contemptuous of success. They seem to have an attitude that you must have done something wrong; you probably succeeded by keeping other people down, by exploiting the poor. Maybe it's because the journalists are not paid much and are envious. He finally agreed to take off the watch. Now, before I go into any editorial board meeting or other meeting with reporters, I do a "Rolex check" for expensive jewelry. I suspect editors expect people in education to wear plain clothes and drive modest cars and that's what I would recommend for these meetings. Ditch the Mercedes.

Pay attention to the details of your clothing and appearance. Dress modestly. You don't want to give them anything to pick at. While you don't want to dress beneath yourself, the editors and reporters may be wearing jeans. The men will almost certainly not be wearing jackets and probably will loosen their ties, if they even wear them. If they have done it first, I take off my jacket and loosen my tie to get in tune with them.

Prepare for the Meeting

They usually want you in and out in thirty minutes; so plan a twenty-minute presentation to leave time for questions. The expert in your group needs to prepare the briefing outline as an opening statement. Use the out-line to make sure you (1) deliver a consistent message, (2) give key rea-sons, (3) provide key facts and figures, and (4) ask for the editorial. The expert should be able to give the overview in five minutes or less, then turn the meeting over to local people.

I recommend introducing them and emphasizing their connection to the community. Give the size of their schools, how many employees, stu-dents, where the students come from, demographics, and so forth. If they have deep roots, mention that. Convince the editors that these people and their issue are important to the newspaper's community.

It's a good idea to hand out a paragraph or two on these people with name, address, phone number, schools, and other pertinent information. You want to make sure the newspaper people have every opportunity to get their facts right, and giving it to them in writing works best.

Role of the Members or Employees

Reassure the two local people that they do not need to become experts on technical aspects of legislation. Often the fear of seeming ignorant keeps them from becoming advocates. Their role is simply to tell the editorial writers how your proposal affects them in the newspaper's community. Generally it is best to leave explaining technical points or discussing poli-tics to the professional.

Use a PR Professional

Have a PR person work with your volunteers to draw out anecdotes, examples, and facts to bring the issue to life in terms of real people. Your PR professional can help them focus on the community and add emotional impact. He or she knows what will appeal to editors and what won't.

Your PR person can train your members or employees to make their most important points in five minutes each. They also need to know it is okay to say, "I don't know. I'd better let (the expert) answer that." A PR person can anticipate questions and coach good answers. It takes me about two hours to work with people, draw out the illuminating anecdotes that make their issue come alive, and coach them to tell their story.

Stories that touch editors emotionally are the most effective. Editors will be moved by an emotional story from their circulation area long before they will be persuaded by your logical case. Basically you can give a good presentation in fifteen minutes, five for the pro and five each for two volunteer advocates.

Magnify the Effect

Merely getting the editorial may not do much good. The targeted politicians may not see it. Even if they do, it's hard to imagine them reading it and changing their minds. So train and organize your advocates in each newspaper market to take the following steps:

1. Tear out the editorial (the whole original sheet, not a copy). Circle the editorial and mail it to targeted politicians with a personal letter.
2. A designated number of individuals, perhaps four or five at spaced intervals, respond with letters to the editor and phone calls to politicians. (See next section.) Any that are published should be mailed to politicians (original pages from the newspaper) with a supportive letter.
3. Provide one member with a ghostwritten, localized article for the op-ed page. This member should be trained to rewrite it on letterhead and deliver it personally, offering it as an article to clarify additional points. It may be necessary to interview this person, draw out examples of his experience, and write it for him. Explain that it's like writing a speech and it's okay to publish something under his name, even though he had help writing it.
4. Appoint someone specific for each newspaper to send you a copy of everything printed. This is necessary because it's hard to track results, particularly if you are on a statewide or national campaign and stimulating lots of coverage. I have never had much success getting the newspaper people to send me things that are published. Often you can check online.
5. Take all editorials, letters, and follow-up material and compile copies into a booklet to give to each targeted politician and to your association board. This is something you may also want to show at your annual convention. The synergy you get from multiple editorials is incredible. The power of a stack of editorials from around the state

or nation, nicely bound, cannot be overstated. I have seen politicians' eyes widen as they flipped through a book of editorials from their district, scanning the headlines and realizing how many people must have seen them. Sometimes they've already seen them piecemeal, but seeing them all at once has a powerful impact.

6. Use the editorial to promote additional news coverage to other editors at that paper, other papers, and television stations. You will see others singing the same tune, particularly if you have scored a positive editorial with an influential newspaper. Many times, they'll just reprint the original editorial.

Letters to the Editor

Call your newspaper and find out what the rules are. Some limit number of letters, length, and so on. Look at the letters they have published. Yours should be about the same size. Give them what they want.

The Letters to the Editor section is one of the most read sections in any newspaper. Having a letter to the editor published can provide information to tens or hundreds of thousands of people. Legislators pay close attention to the letters that appear in their local papers and usually have someone on staff monitoring them. Sometimes they hire a commercial service. Even if your letter is not selected for publication, submitting it can make a difference as editors of the letters section gauge how their readers feel about an issue by how many letters they receive for and against. Either way, writing a letter can have a huge impact.

Follow these steps for writing a letter to the editor:

1. Decide on your message. Newspapers usually publish letters that respond to a recently published article, opinion piece, or editorial. Search the paper daily for stories about incidents related to your message or respond to stories and editorials your association has generated.

2. Write your letter. Write your letter quickly, the sooner the better: The first letters received on a topic are read first and more likely to be selected. Write as if you're talking to the editor of the newspaper in person. Cite the article to which you are responding, including the date, or refer to the fact your legislation is near a decision step.

Timeliness is important, so make it clear your letter is relevant to something about to happen or that just happened or was reported.

3. Cite personal experiences. One topic per letter. Concentrate on a few powerful points, maybe just one. Avoid personal attacks. Addressing ideas expressed by others can make for a lively letter; attacking individuals makes you look petty.

4. Keep it short. There is an average limit of 250 words for letters; some papers have shorter limits. Longer letters are less likely to be published and, if selected, will almost definitely be edited. Don't let the letters editor remove or dilute your most important points.

5. Submit your letter. Proofread and check spelling. Have a friend read it over to double-check that everything looks good. It should be easy to read it out loud. Use your real name. Newspapers do not print anonymous letters.

6. Include your phone numbers for confirmation and a regular mailing address, even if you are submitting by e-mail. Newspapers need this information for internal use to confirm that you are the person who submitted the letter. They will usually print the name of your town, but not your actual address or phone number.

7. Call and find out their preferred method for you to submit your letter by fax, e-mail, or regular mail. Send it and call to confirm they have it. If you submit by e-mail, paste your letter into the text of the e-mail. Do not send attachments. Many papers will not open an e-mail with an attachment.

8. Start off strong. Make your first sentence a grabber. Present your viewpoint or offer a new way to consider the issue. Include a few striking facts that might surprise an editor or a reader. Make it relevant to the newspaper's circulation area and readers. Tell the editors, readers, and elected officials what you want them to do!

9. Use the letter. Tear out the page the letter runs on, circle it, and send it to the elected officials you want to influence. They may not see it otherwise. Include a letter reiterating or expanding your key points. Send a copy of the letter to the group that encouraged you to write or to the group that is working on your topic so that the organization can follow the bigger picture.

11

Money: A Moral, Ethical, Legal, Effective Tool to Achieve Your Goals

MONEY: THE BAD RAP

Many educators feel awkward and uneasy about money and politics. Principals, administrators, and school board members, unlike some other groups, aren't used to using money to achieve political goals. Like many Americans, they read in the newspaper and see on TV how political action committees influence members of Congress, how people with the biggest PACs seem to get what they want, how money can determine who gets elected, and that the PACs have the money. It looks like something you don't want to be part of.

I doubt educators will ever use money in a big way. It might even be counterproductive to try. But it's important to understand that money does have a role in politics and to see how it is used—what it can do and what it cannot do.

As you consider money and politics, ask this question: Do you want to work within the system or try to change it? If you want to change the system, you will have a lot of company among professional lobbyists and corporate and association executives. Many find the practice of raising and distributing money distasteful. Many people in Congress and the states want to change the way we finance elections.

The problem is, no one has been able to come up with a better way that people will support. Given that it costs a lot of money to communicate to voters and we want to have elections, a lot of money has to be raised from somewhere. Quite a few state house and senate races are now costing more than $1 million. Few people can afford that, so candidates have to raise money wherever they can.

You can make a strong case for publicly financing elections. For $10 to $50 per citizen, depending on how much reform you want to buy, we could pay for elections. But not enough people want to do that, so what we have is a system of privatized elections. It's almost like raising money in the stock market. Candidates have to make the case and persuade people to invest in something they believe in. So in a very real sense, the system makes sure only people with support can run.

By contrast, we pay for police, fire, and health departments; we pay for juries, judges, and prosecutors; we even pay senators, representatives, governors, and presidents, once they are elected. But to get elected, they have to beg and borrow from people whose main interest is getting something in return. Don't blame the people who run for office or the people who give them money for behaving the way they do. All of us are operating in the system taxpayers could change tomorrow, if they wanted to.

Whatever you think, my goal is to help you work within the system. Incidentally, these techniques can help you change the system, if that's what you want. It's good to remember that political action committees (PACs) *are* the reform. They were created by Congress and the states to shine light on the flow of money into campaigns. By and large it has worked. We have a system of campaign finance that is transparent and honest. It used to be much worse.

I had a conversation with a retired banker from Georgia a few years back. He told me part of his job had been to act as the political "bagman." He took the gym bags full of cash over to the capitol in Atlanta. He did not actually go into the governor's office; he went off to the side. One of the staff people would take the bag and thank him. He said he had delivered as much as $50,000 in cash at a time—many times—this way.

The record is clear that influence used to be bought that way, with cash passed under the table. In the case of Georgia Senator Herman Talmadge, persons unknown to him used to put large bills in his suit coat pockets—much to his amazement. I'm not saying it doesn't happen anymore, but it's a lot cleaner than it used to be and the PAC system is the reason why.

PAC money is honest, legal money, reported and on the record, and those records are available for anyone to look at. For now, money to run campaigns will continue to come mostly from individuals writing private checks, whether to politicians directly or to PACs. (Some states allow corporate contributions, and, interestingly, they don't seem to have any better or worse government than the others. But that's another story.)

The major objection many people have is that a PAC contribution feels like an attempt to buy a vote. Having talked to hundreds of PAC money recipients, both state and federal, and to the people who give out the money, I don't think you can buy a vote. At least not with PAC money, which is in the public record. I did have one politician say, in a public meeting, that the money does influence his thinking. He said it is a lot easier to vote with the people who have given money than those who haven't.

His comments affirm what I have said: Many times politicians don't really care which way an issue goes, and it really doesn't matter that much to the public interest, so they vote with their friends. I respect his candor, and I suspect that is true for all elected officials. I still say PAC money cannot buy a vote for a couple of important reasons. One is very practical: The limits on PAC contributions mean that even if a vote were for sale, you couldn't give enough through a PAC.

Another reason is that, in all probability, your opponents have given money to the same people you have. Generally speaking, all the players engaged are giving money and the money tends to balance out or cancel out. This brings up another important reason to give! If your opponents are giving and you aren't . . . who cares more about the issue and about the elected official?

REASONS TO GIVE TO YOUR PAC

The PAC is the most efficient and effective way to raise campaign money from a wide base of contributors. It's an efficient and effective way to make your voice heard in the legislature and Congress. In fact it is very hard to present a credible political presence without a PAC. If you have no PAC, you may not be taken seriously. You just don't look like a serious organization. If you want to be heard, it helps to have a PAC.

1. Working together, we have more impact than all of us working separately. The money we give is pooled so it has more impact. Former Senator David Boren of Oklahoma once pointed out—in opposing PACs—that the average U.S. senator must raise $13,000 a week for six years to finance the next election. (The number is higher today.) "If people come in to see you and one is a student and one is a small businessman and one is a teacher and one is a farmer and one is a PAC person with big campaign contributions, who are you going to see in your limited time?" he asked. Of course, the answer is that many of those farmers and teachers and small business people had contributed personally and to a PAC, and so . . .

Some of us, when we give money to candidates, will give $100, $250, or maybe $500. But a contribution of that size is rare. Most people will give less than $100. Candidates value those and like to brag that they are getting lots of small contributions. With the advent of the Internet, raising enough small contributions to fund a campaign may become possible at the national or presidential level. But while candidates love to get those small contributions, they are expensive to recruit; they can't remember the contributors and don't even know who they are. Therefore, the key to influential giving is to give enough to rise out of the herd and get noticed. By pulling together those small contributions into a large PAC check from your association, you can have a major impact and your association will be remembered and appreciated.

2. Unlike most of us who only pay attention to politics during the election campaigns, the PAC is eternally vigilant. It keeps an eye on elected officials and issues all year round, and can take action as needed and keep you informed.

3. The PAC allows us to hold elected officials accountable. If they don't support us, we won't support them. We may support their opponent. There is a subtle but real effect on politicians when they know you have a huge war chest you can throw into elections or issue fights. Usually they would like to avoid a fight, and certainly an expensive one. The thought that you might go public and oppose them can have a powerful deterrent effect.

One political operative told me this story: There was a member of Congress from Pennsylvania who consistently opposed his union clients on an issue involving the National Labor Relations Board. Finally they decided they had to do something serious to get the congressman to change his position. They prepared a series of radio ads to run in the district explaining the congressman's stand and the effect on people in the district (from the union's point of view, of course).

They went to the congressman and told him they didn't want to run the ads and they didn't want to get into a fight, but they were prepared to if he couldn't compromise. They played the ads for him. He blinked. Rather than get into a fight with a well-financed opponent, he cut a deal. Having a well-stocked PAC is like having missiles in a silo: You may never have to fire them to get the benefit.

4. PAC money has more impact because it is easier to get. Candidates have to spend money to raise money from individuals, but PAC money comes in large lump sums. Unless you are Howard Dean or some other famous politician, it's almost impossible to run a campaign on money raised in $25 and $50 contributions. It's too expensive to get each one and you use all your money raising money.

5. PAC contributions give candidates a clear idea of where you stand on the issue. When you give personal money, usually the only thing they know is that you like them personally. A personal contribution may be misunderstood. The PAC money represents a specific interest, not just an individual. That interest—or rather its PAC—has carefully considered which candidates to support. That interest group is permanent; it was here last year and it'll be here next year—as will the possibility of support or opposition.

6. The PAC expands your influence beyond your own political district. It directs your money to candidates you may not know about throughout the state and nation who need your support. I seldom encounter a person who sends a personal check to a distant district, to a candidate for whom he cannot vote, unless it's someone running for president.

What if the person running for office from your district is adamantly opposed to your interest? Or just doesn't care? Or is weak and can't help? You won't give, but how can you identify those people who support your views? The PAC knows. The PAC looks around the whole state and nation and applies your money where it will do the most good.

7. The PAC makes a carefully studied, well-informed decision on who to support. Many things go on in Congress and the legislature that people outside the process don't know about. The PAC and your lobbyists support and oppose candidates based on inside knowledge of what really happened to your issues.

This differs significantly from the way personal donations are decided. Givers often don't know much about a candidate's voting record or competency in matters that don't show up in votes. My experience has been that the most important factor in whether people contribute personal money is whether they know and like a candidate. One reason is that most of us don't have the time or interest to focus on what our elected officials do in office. We don't know all the different ways and occasions they may have acted for or against our interest.

One state representative in Florida told this story to a group of realtors I was training. He explained that he was a banker and served on several committees relating to banking and finance. Having been there some years, he carried a lot of clout. The realtors had supported him and he considered himself their friend. The realtors were supporting a bill that came up in one of his committees that related to finance. Although he had some reservations about the bill, they weren't serious, and so, because of his friendship, he said nothing. "I could have killed that bill, but I sat on my hands," he said. His point was that this action—or inaction—was not something that would show up in voting records, but it was important.

Most of us are unlikely to know about such actions and unlikely to support someone far from our home district who helps us this way. But the PAC knows.

8. *The PAC makes its decisions based only on your issues as decided by the membership and leadership of your association.* Sometimes it will support a candidate that some members don't like because of her stand on unrelated issues. That's because the PAC is designed to support only narrow issues. For example, an elected official may support charter schools. Maybe she is a Democrat and you are a Republican. Your personal feelings on those issues may not allow you to give money to that candidate. But that same candidate may have consistently supported budget increases and other issues that help you. Maybe she is the chair of a key committee. (Incidentally, you can learn a lot from the realtors, who are politically effective. They like to say they are not for the Republican Party or the Democratic Party: They are for the Realtor Party.)

The PAC will make a cold, calculated investment to protect your interest, one you might not make because of the conflicting issues. The PACs I work with that are most successful, and the ones I set up operate systematically and dispassionately to evaluate candidates.

You have a local and perhaps a state and national committee that considers candidates and elected officials already in office. They go through a rigorous process of evaluating what candidates have said and done, their electability, and their understanding of issues.

They try hard to separate out the stands on social issues, political parties, and other factors not relevant to the narrow focus of the organization. They ask, "Which candidate is best for this special interest?" and then invest your money where it will represent you the best.

9. PACs are legally established by the legislature and Congress. The purpose is to establish an open, honest regulated system by which people can join together to support or oppose candidates. The PAC system allows the public to know who contributes and who receives money. PACs are one way we have chosen to finance elections.

10. The PAC is an important education device for elected officials. Properly done, the process by which your association decides who will get PAC money becomes an important communication medium to elected officials. I learned this when I ran for state house of representatives in my home state of North Carolina. Only one PAC was interested in my race. It was a coalition of builders, realtors, apartment companies, and developers. They sent around a person who lived and worked in my district with a long questionnaire. On the surface, the purpose was to find out how I felt about the issues they were concerned with.

It was a real eye-opener for me. I had no idea how to answer many of the questions, although it was clear I needed to know the answers if I were to be effective after I was elected. In answering their questions, I had to ask for more information and think hard about what I heard. It was an introduction to a lot of issues and information I had never had access to.

When I set up PAC committees for my clients, I recommend a formal process in which a committee screens all candidates. This way you get a dialogue between the committee and the candidates. When candidates are appealing for money from your PAC, they will learn about your association and your issues better than at any other time.

11. Your PAC is an important tool to protect your specific education interest. It is designed and operates to protect your right to operate schools the way you want to. When you think about whether to give and how much, ask yourself, "What is it worth to get the results I want?" People in oil marketing, banking, logging, fishing, and many other industries have awakened to find their ability to stay in business compromised by a failure to pay attention to the political climate they operate in. The same thing can happen to issues in education you care about. Giving to your PAC makes sure someone is looking after you and your interest. Former Wyoming Senator Alan Simpson was talking about grassroots involvement, but he summed it up well when he said, "Take part or get taken apart."

12

Key Contacts: The Only System That Works

THE ONE AND ONLY SYSTEM THAT WORKS FOR MOST ISSUES: KEY CONTACTS

The most successful advocacy organizations have adopted a "key contact" grassroots system: The association selects a member who lives and works in the district (or state for U.S. senators) to be the key contact. This is someone willing to build a supportive, trusting relationship and deliver the association's message as needed.

This contrasts with broad-based systems in which the association has a list of names and sends action alerts to everyone. The difference is significant. Most organizations that think they have a grassroots operation have only a database of names. They have no idea when people communicate or how effectively. Even organizations that use Internet systems, and there are plenty of good ones, often aren't much better off even though they can track the communications.

Yes, I know Howard Dean energized a great many people. I know MoveOn.org has mobilized millions. But your issues are not the same and will not be resolved the same way. Nor do you have the capacity to mobilize tens of thousands of people. And you don't need to. Look at the difference from a politician's viewpoint:

Key Contact: Message comes from a known, trusted person
Broad Based: Message from unknowns, perhaps faked

KC: Often delivered face-to-face
BB: Usually e-mail, easily dismissed, ignored, and discounted

KC: Message detailed, tailored to the person and the moment
BB: Message is repetitive, canned, minimal, simplistic

KC: Depends on persuasion, logic, mutual benefit
BB: Depends on volume

KC: Provides two-way communication, feedback, and response
BB: One way or with only form letters exchanged

KC: Focused, efficient, targets only specific decision makers
BB: Shotgun, hit or miss, wastes effort

KC: Politicians and staff appreciate input from constituents
BB: Mass campaigns cause problems and are resented

KC: Committed person willing to invest time and energy
BB: Minimal investment in e-mail means minimal concern

A key-contact system will serve you and your association best. It is a system, an organization, a campaign, not just a list. It is action versus hope. It is accountability versus guesswork. A key-contact system is based on these concepts:

- Recruit, train, and support specific people to build long-term relationships with politicians
- Maximize effort by targeting key decision makers in Congress and the legislature first and foremost
- Support those politicians personally and organizationally with help of many kinds, especially money

When setting up a key-contact system, it's a good idea to spell out your expectations in writing or else people will create their own. In that case, they may perceive the job to be much more or much less than you actually want.

Here's a sample job description adapted from associations I have worked with. It tells you what is usually expected of a key contact. If your organization doesn't have a job description for volunteer advocates, maybe this will help you develop one.

Administrators Association Key Contact Job Description

General Responsibilities:
Key contact agrees to build and maintain strong, positive relationships

with assigned members of the United States Senate and House of Representatives and contact them as requested and deliver PAC check.

Specific Objectives:

Key contact is responsible for staying abreast of association legislative priorities and initiatives through association government relations mailings, Internet postings, and the newsletter.

Key contact is to meet personally with a designated legislator at least two times a year to review priority legislative issues.

Key contact is to invite legislator to visit school for information session and photo op at least annually.

Key contact is to deliver PAC campaign check to assigned legislator as necessary.

Key contact is to attend local meetings with association staff as needed. This includes attendance at the annual association government relations summer group meetings and probably local political meetings the assigned legislator attends.

Communicating Issues:

Key contact is to respond to requests for contact as indicated in legislative alerts. Action requested may consist of writing a letter, coordinating a letter-writing campaign, making a personal visit, or calling a legislator.

Reporting:

Key contact is to promptly report back to government relations staff (by faxing the response form, e-mail, or telephone) on contacts made; report should include any legislator comments on issues discussed.

Key contact is expected to participate in political action committee with a leadership contribution, personal contribution, and volunteer time.

Appendix A

How You Gonna Call? Effectiveness
Rating for Forms of Communication

100   Eyeball to eyeball; it's hard to say no when you're looking someone in the eye

98   Personal letter/fax (with a handwritten note on it) or e-mail (your
own words, localized to the official's district or state if she knows
you and it's personalized and you confirm a decision maker read
it)

93   Thoughtful phone call with dialogue

85   Fax (personalized and you confirm it was received)

80   Meeting with senior staff

40   Phone call with instructions to vote yes or no, leaving your name

40   Meeting with junior staff

30   Obviously orchestrated impersonal communication in any form
(gang phone calls from a convention, stimulated form telegrams,
e-mails, faxes, etc., even with names of individuals in the district)

20   E-mail, if she doesn't know you

15   Preprinted anything (form letter, postcard, issue paper, fax)

10   Petitions (no matter how many signatures)

0   Anything from outside the district, unless you represent a national
or state organization with people in the district or are communicating to a committee chair or committee staff, in which case it
could go as high as 80.

Everything you do to communicate with elected officials has some
impact—preprinted postcards, petitions, e-mail, form letters—everything.
But as you move down the scale of impact from in person to remote and
impersonal, it has geometrically diminishing impact.

Members of Congress and state legislatures are buried in mail, phone calls, faxes, and e-mail they will never see. They barely have enough staff to handle all the stuff that comes in, much less give it consideration. If you look at congressional websites, they all tell you to communicate only with your own elected official—the one you can vote for.

So focus on and multiply things we know have maximum impact. Personal, eyeball-to-eyeball relationships followed up and reinforced by thoughtful, permanent written communication are about the only things that can penetrate the tidal wave of messages flowing into politicians' offices. One chief of staff from a Washington office told me his member sometimes would meet with twenty people in a day. On top of all the other work members do, can you imagine how hard it is to remember any of this?

Your relationship with the politician and staff is probably the most important determinant whether you get a response. If you doubt that, here is a list compiled by Bill Posey, who served in the Florida House of Representatives and now serves in the senate. He's an effective legislator and, unlike many, willing to tell it like it is. The difference between part-time state legislators will small or no staff and members of Congress is evident.

POSEY'S PRACTICAL POINTERS FOR EFFECTIVE GRASSROOTS LOBBYING ON A REALITY SCALE OF 1 TO 10

- 1 point   Send photocopied letters
- 2 points   Send out faxes on hot issues
- 3 points   Send copy of monthly magazine or newsletter
- 4 points   Call the legislative office
- 5 + points   Send personal letters, regardless of quality
- − 2 points   Call them at their regular/real job about legislation
- − 5 points   Call them at home
- − 10 points   Call them at home late at night
- 2 to 8 points   Present high ratings or awards depending upon quality and prestige

Meet personally by appointment to discuss positions and issues:

- 10 points   If you are a voter in the district
- 10 points   If you are a contributor

- 10 points   If you are both of the above
- 1 point   If you are none of the above
- − 10 points   If you supported opponent and it was a nasty campaign (stay away until you are in a position to offer support next time)
- 1 point   When discussing business over dinner, use the opportunity to build relationships (in most cases, $1,000 lobster dinners won't buy support for your issues, regardless of what the press says)

Appendix B

Seven Steps for Creating a
Powerful In-Person Encounter

CHECKLIST FOR DELIVERING YOUR MESSAGE

When you visit an elected official, certain things will increase your effectiveness. This is a seven-step checklist for a successful meeting.

1. Tell him who you are: Not just your name and title, but a little about yourself, your schools, your students, your personal history, and your family. You want him to know you as a human being, not just an issue advocate. Make sure he knows you represent an association, not just yourself, so he connects your visit to your professional lobbyist.
2. Anecdote/story: Bring your issue to life in human terms. Tell about real children, parents, and teachers from the politician's state or district who are or will be affected. Think "soap opera" with details, names, dates, and places; make it come alive.
3. What you want: Make sure the politician knows exactly what you came for: vote yes, vote no, cosponsor, speak to someone on the committee, and so on.
4. Why it's a good idea: Have at least three sound reasons why this elected official should support your position, especially focusing on the impact in his state or district.
5. Ask for support: Look directly in his eyes, lock on, and ask, "Will you vote with us (write the letter, cosponsor, or whatever)?"
6. Remember thank-you notes: Send handwritten notes to everyone you talk with.
7. Report results: Always detail the results of the meeting back to the headquarters of your association.

Appendix C

Be-Attitudes to Help You Succeed,
Persevere, and Recover

BE-ATTITUDES

Be Practical

If legislators make a reasonable request, try to comply with it. Do not back away for fear that it is a "deal" or that you are "getting into politics."

Be Realistic

Most legislation is the result of compromise. It always has been and always will be in a democracy. Do not expect that everything will go your way, and do not be critical when it does not. Avoid blaming your legislators for "failing" to do what you want. The failure may be yours. Make certain first that you did a good job presenting your case.

Be Generous

Give credit where credit is due. If an issue goes the way you want, remember that legislators always deserve first credit because their votes decided the issue. Remember also that on all the big issues, many organizations and individuals may have participated on your side. Do your part to make certain that credit is shared by all of them.

Be Understanding

Recognize that each legislator has commitments and that a certain amount of vote trading goes on in a legislature. Just because a legislator votes against you doesn't mean you've been deserted. She may just disagree. She may have felt more pressure from the other side. She may have felt this vote earned a credit for something in the future. When your friends vote against you, it generally means they owe you one and you will be able to call in that chit in the future. You do have the right to ask for an explanation of votes and to express your disappointment.

Be a Good Opponent

Fight issues, not people. Remember the old adage, We have no permanent friends and no permanent enemies, only permanent interests. Today's opponents may be tomorrow's allies, and that will work if you have remained respectful adversaries.

Be Reliable

Stick to your word. If it ever becomes necessary to back down on a promise, explain why and make sure they hear it from you first. People can understand and accept that things change, but they will never forgive or forget a double-cross, even if unintentional.

Be Not Misled

Almost everyone who talks to an elected official gets a polite reception. Do not mistake friendliness for friendship. "I'll give it careful consideration," says nothing and may be a kiss-off. My rule: Yes means yes, no means no, and nothing else means anything. You have the right to press for a commitment, and they have the right to hold their cards close to the chest and avoid commitment pending further information.

One way around this little dance is to ask, "I understand you might not be able to make a commitment, but how do you feel about this based on what you know now?" Then you can follow with "What additional information do you need before you make a decision?" (And provide it.)

Another good line is "When may I call to check back?" Whatever your politician says, follow up relentlessly, respectfully, and politely. Sometimes it can take weeks for her to explore your issue since she may have to check with various committees and other people inside and outside the legislature. You don't want to irritate her, but it's probably not too much to call every two weeks or so to let her know you haven't gone away. If you waver or falter, you give her permission to ignore you. A measure of success is when she tells you to back off, meaning that she has heard you.

Be Persistent

The fat lady never sings in politics. Win or lose, it's never over. You can always come back. Your opponents can always come back. Any major piece of legislation will take five to eight years to pass and longer to implement. So you must never give up.

Appendix D

Letters, E-mails, Faxes, and How to Make Them Work

The single most powerful weapon in your political arsenal is a letter. Not just any letter, but a special sort of letter. Given the security measures in place, sending postal mail is no longer a good option for Congress, so "letter" includes fax and e-mail. But sending something that looks like an ordinary e-mail will cause your communication to be discounted by many people in Congress. So think about sending a pdf document that looks like letterhead and contains an inklike signature. It may be printed and given to the member of Congress to carry outside the office, read on the plane, and so on. You can also use html to create an e-mail that looks like letterhead. Whatever you do, realize that appearances are important. Ordinary e-mails make less of an impression than something more businesslike.

Considering all I've said about how elected officials want to hear from their constituents, I strongly recommend you indicate you are one up front. This means in the subject line of an e-mail and the first line of an e-mail, fax, or letter, you say something like "I live in District [XX]," giving the correct number for the district your official serves. For the U.S. Senate, "I live in [City] and [State]." If there is any way, make a personal connection. "You probably don't remember, but we shook hands at the barbecue last August in Des Moines."

Why write? Letters take more effort than a phone call and require you to get your thoughts in order. They are permanent. They can be copied. They go into files by issue. They are hard to ignore.

As you set out to influence your government, put it in writing. As you write, remember that, to be special, your letter must be thoughtful and personal. That is not to say that form letters don't have any impact. They do. When enough people send in letters saying essentially the same thing, using the same words, elected officials know they are part of an organized campaign. The fact that they know it's organized is not only okay—it's necessary. You need to be part of something larger than one person to get attention.

However, to truly change the mind or vote of an elected official, you need to appeal not only to their political instincts but also to their reason and emotion. They are interested in who is touched by your issue and how they are affected. How will it play out for their constituents? They are interested in who cares and how much you care and why you care. They are interested in whether you know what you are talking about and have anything worthwhile to say. Consider the following letter (name omitted). This was given to me, rather proudly, by a nursing home administrator. Read it and see what you think the politician's reaction would be.

Re: $29 million cut in Medicaid
Dear Governor,

Apparently, sir, you have forgotten that the elderly in today's Florida nursing homes are those citizens who just a few years ago either fought, farmed, worked in industries, paid dearly for lost loved ones and paid taxes for World War I, II, Korea, and Vietnam. After the world wars, they paid for our hospitals, constructed universities, built interstates, fed other nations, and are directly responsible for all these contributions to the greatest nation that exists.

Today, after their strength has been spent and finances exhausted, they live hopelessly with their last days at the mercy of unappreciative politicians.

How can elected officials conscientiously live with themselves and their conscience, day after day spending billions after billions of American dollars for projects all over the world and failing to provide adequate funds for our own?

Cuts of $29 million, plus no increase in Medicaid rates for the care of Florida's infirm elderly, are absolutely uncalled for.

Governor, you can do better.

The next few months will tell all Floridians if you are a responsible person, the man who supports the health and welfare of the elderly, sick, and infirm, or just another heartless politician.

As a lifetime Democrat, I pray that you will come to your senses and act responsibly.

Sincerely,
John Doe

At first glance, many people like this letter. However, consider the tone. What does this writer think about politicians—about the governor? What is the governor likely to remember from this letter? Would a staff person pass this on to the governor? If the governor did see this, I suspect the words "heartless politician" may hang heavy in his mind. I also suspect the governor does not see himself as a "heartless politician."

The only reason this letter gives him to change his mind is that one slightly upset person will think he's heartless. It is personal, but is it thoughtful? Does it cause the reader to stop and think? A letter needs to give specific reasons to support your position, just like an in-person meeting. For example, what if the writer had said:

> I'm writing to urge you to restore the $29 million in proposed Medicaid cuts. I realize you face tough choices in balancing the state budget. But I am worried that if the funds for Medicaid are cut further, the steps we will have to take to economize on the cost of care will be harmful to our elderly nursing home residents.
>
> I've been an administrator for twenty-seven years. In my nursing home we are certified for 150 beds and usually they are all filled. The state pays us $88 a day to give near-hospital-level care to elderly residents. While we will always find ways to provide adequate care, if you cut the already meager funding we have, we will have to consider cutting some things that make a major difference in the quality of life our elderly enjoy. For example, under your proposed budget we have to consider cutting:
>
> 1. Trips to the mall for our mobile elderly. We take them once a week and for many it is their only contact with the outside world other than television.
> 2. Premium canned beans. We can cut back by using the canned beans with ends in them, although they often cause problems for elderly with dentures.
> 3. Staff. We have more aides on duty than the state requires because when an old person wants a drink of water, we want him or her to be able to get it promptly. At state minimums, an aide may care for ten residents and just can't get to them often enough.
>
> There is more, and I invite you to come to our nursing home and see for yourself. We provide excellent care on the funds we receive, and in fact,

nursing homes provide the most efficient and cost-effective care of any institutions in the state.

But we are in danger of falling back to merely adequate custodial care because of rising expenses and reduced funding. The proposed budget cuts of $29 million in Medicaid will substantially reduce the quality of life for our elderly in nursing homes. I hope you will look carefully for other ways to balance the budget and restore the cuts as proposed by the Southern Association of Nursing Homes.

Please let me know your feelings about this as soon as possible. If you want more information, I will be glad to provide it.

This version is designed to show sympathy for the governor, who has to make tough choices, and to give enough specifics to show the effect of budget cuts. The beans, the mall trip, the glass of water—all are designed to conjure up specific images. They are real examples given to me when I questioned nursing home administrators about what would happen if the Medicaid budget were cut.

Which letter do you think would have a more positive impact?

The second letter mentions the association, so the governor knows the letter is part of a widespread campaign. Notice it also tells something of the experience and position of the writer. Remember, you are an expert in your area. It's important to let the elected official know you are knowledgeable. Enough letters like this, thoughtful and personal, to governors and legislators or the residents and members of Congress, can have dramatic effect.

It helps if you let the recipient know you are politically savvy. When communicating with senators and representatives, state the number of their district and tell them you are a member of an association. Tell them

What you want.
Where your issue is in the process.
When the next action step is likely.
What the effect is on real people in your schools.

Keep it short. One page is enough. If you have more to say, put it in another letter and send it later. If you don't get a reply within ten days, call and ask what happened to your letter. You may have to send it again. But don't quit until you get an answer.

If you get an answer and don't like it, write again and ask for a conversation, saying this issue is really important to you.

AND YET . . .

Over the years I have said, and almost everyone else in the business has said, a one-page letter is best. That's certainly true if you are trying to show that you, someone known and respected, is taking a stand. But I'm not sure that one page is best if you are trying to persuade someone to change his or her mind.

My thinking on this started to change while I was standing in the office of Texas State Representative Patricia Gray with some folks from her district. As we talked, she noticed the name tag of a man with us and said, "You sent me a letter, didn't you?" She explained that she had not responded yet because she was still thinking about the issues raised in the letter.

In my mind, the fact she remembered it and was thinking about it was significant. She was chair of the Sunset Commission, which was reviewing laws to decide which should be retained, changed, or eliminated. I was so struck by the moment I got permission to reprint the following exchange of letters. First, the one to her:

The Honorable Patricia Gray
Texas House of Representatives
P.O. Box 2910
Austin, Texas 78769

Dear Representative Gray:
    The Texas Credit Union Commission is going through the Sunset review process this session.
    There are various proposals to change the agency's governance and renewal term. I believe the proposals would be adverse to the agency's effectiveness because they emanate from the interests of banking groups. The banking industry is engaged in an aggressive campaign to thwart the ongoing development and success of credit unions.
    Please consider that the Credit Union Commission has been an effective regulatory body since 1969. It should be renewed for another 12 years—not for only 4 years as urged by banking interests.

Also, the commission's structure of 6 industry members and 3 public members has worked effectively since 1983 when the public members were added. That structure should be kept intact because it has proven to be effective.

Finally, there is a proposal to complicate the commission's existing administrative procedures with burdensome hearings for handling matters, such as charter and bylaw amendments. These matters have been effectively and fairly administered in the past. Such unnecessary hearings would unduly hamper the orderly development of credit unions.

Please give careful consideration to these matters. We want to be able to continue giving good service to our members.

Sincerely,
Roger McCrary
Chairman of the Board

This letter reads quickly, but it is a little longer than one page. It got the following response:

Dear Mr. McCrary,

Thank you for writing my office regarding your concerns for the Credit Union Commission. I am very supportive of the concept of credit unions and the invaluable service and access they provide to the community.

As you may know, on Tuesday, September 24, the Sunset Commission formally met to vote on the proposed recommendations affecting the structure of the Texas Credit Union Commission. The Sunset Commission voted to maintain the Credit Union Commission's autonomy; however, we recommended they comply with some public notice and comment before their hearings regarding approval or denial of charter applications, field membership expansion, and mergers.

The Sunset Commission also voted to improve the public's representation on the Credit Union Commission's Board, which is a policy that every state agency must comply with to ensure the public receives adequate input. The Sunset Commission did not recommend consolidating the Credit Union Commission with the Finance Commission, since the Finance Commission will not be reviewed by the Sunset Commission for possible restructuring until 2001.

I am frankly at a loss to understand how these two very mild changes will undermine credit unions in Texas. I respectfully disagree that all is completely rosy with the regulation of credit unions. The Sunset review found that one-quarter of the state-regulated credit unions had financial problems serious enough to warrant a remedial monitoring program. Only twenty of those improved enough to be removed from remedial monitoring by the end of the year assessed.

Once again, I appreciate your taking the time to write my office regarding your thoughts on the Credit Union Commission.

Sincerely,
Patricia Gray

I like this exchange, even though the writer did not get what he wanted. Representative Gray gave careful consideration to his letter but just disagreed. Getting the politician to think is more than half the battle.